# Trauma and Documentary Photography of the FSA

Defining Moments in American Photography

Anthony W. Lee, Editor

1. *On Alexander Gardner's "Photographic Sketch Book" of the Civil War,* by Anthony W. Lee and Elizabeth Young

2. *Lynching Photographs,* by Dora Apel and Shawn Michelle Smith, with an introduction by Anthony W. Lee

3. *Weegee and "Naked City,"* by Anthony W. Lee and Richard Meyer

4. *"The Steerage" and Alfred Stieglitz,* by Jason Francisco and Elizabeth Anne McCauley, with an introduction by Anthony W. Lee

5. *Trauma and Documentary Photography of the FSA,* by Sara Blair and Eric Rosenberg, with an introduction by Anthony W. Lee

# Trauma and Documentary Photography of the FSA

SARA BLAIR

ERIC ROSENBERG

*Published with the assistance of The Getty Foundation*

University of California Press
Berkeley Los Angeles London

The publisher gratefully acknowledges the generous contribution to this book provided by the Art Endowment Fund of the University of California Press Foundation, which is supported by a major gift from the Ahmanson Foundation.

# Contents

# Introduction

Anthony W. Lee

INITIALLY KNOWN AS THE RESETTLEMENT ADMINISTRATION, the Farm Security Administration (FSA) was an umbrella organization established by the United States government during the Great Depression to combat the problem of rural poverty. Devoted to "rural rehabilitation," it aimed its programs chiefly at tenant farmers, sharecroppers, and the poorest landowners. Among many other (then-controversial) activities, it bought up bad farms and promoted agricultural collectives, offered training in the latest farming techniques, resettled families from the most wretched of the Dust Bowl's dried-up parcels, built migrant camps, established health clinics that provided free medical care, and loaned money to tenant farmers so that they could become landowners outright.[1] At its height, it operated in nearly all forty-eight states, had more than 2,300 branch offices, employed some 19,000 people, and served more than 850,000 "clients," as the farmers were called.

The FSA's social achievements were considerable by almost any measure. But although it saved nearly a million American farmers from starvation with its various programs and helped to transform the nature of government intervention in agriculture, the FSA is today arguably known less for its social or relief work than for its small photographic division, headed by a single man, Roy Stryker, who hired a handful of photographers to document rural Americans and the New Deal's efforts to help them. Indeed, most casual observers, then and now, could not easily name any of the long list of FSA programs or its lead officials, much less its 19,000 full-time employees, but they could probably name its most famous photographers, among them Esther Bubley, Jack Delano, Walker Evans, Dorothea Lange, Russell Lee, Gordon Parks, Arthur Rothstein, Ben Shahn, John Vachon, and Marion Post Wolcott. Their finest pictures, including Lange's *Migrant Mother* and Rothstein's *Dust Storm,* are among the most recognizable images in the history of American photography.

Charged to provide evidence that would help justify the agency's role to a skeptical public, the photographers hired by the FSA began picturing the extraordinary trauma visited upon common people who were struggling daily with displacement, homelessness, and hunger. Distributed widely and shown in museum exhibitions, newspapers, magazines, books, and government reports, the photographs gave thoughtful accounts of the Dust Bowl farms and migrant camps, the Far West and Deep South, and the fields and back roads throughout the country. They showed scenes of poverty and deprivation and of the successes of FSA programs in ameliorating them. Occasionally augmented by charts and captions but just as often presented on their own, the photographs represented a common belief in the power of the camera to make the horrors of the Great Depression instantly visible and to freeze the relentless flow of tragic events as iconic images. In these photographers' hands, and in contrast to the modish habits of an earlier generation of street photographers, the camera's power was to *document.*

Certainly the urge to document was not limited to photographers or to the FSA. As part of much larger cultural project to represent the difficult conditions of the Depression, it could be found in journalistic reporting, newsreels, interviews, realist and proletarian fiction, guidebooks from the Works Progress Administration, films, radio broadcasts, theater, and even music.[2] During the 1930s, documentary was, as William Stott has argued, a full-blown genre as recognizable and as distinct as tragedy, epic, or satire. It was characterized by an effort to convey "knowledge of public facts," as Stott has written, "but sharpen it with feeling; put us in touch with the perennial human spirit, but show it struggling in a particular social context at a specific historical moment."[3] The effort to represent the human experience of such difficult historical circumstances ranged across different media and political persuasions. But arguably it was in photographs that the "documentary idea," as it was sometimes called, found its most potent form of expression.[4] Something about the camera's dual nature—its effortless recording of everyday detail combined with its users' point of view and skill—met the demand for both "facts" and "feeling" and gave it a leg up on other media. Photographers were not alone in believing this. As the writer James Agee famously declared in 1936, "The camera seems to me, next to unassisted and weaponless consciousness, the central instrument of our time."[5] In that way of thinking, the photograph was as close to unvarnished (plain, honest, simple, naked, sincere) representation as was then possible.

But, as is now common knowledge, the idea of the documentary photograph was neither so clear-cut nor straightforward, neither so transparent nor "unassisted" as the New Dealers of the FSA liked to proclaim, and certainly never as programmatically pursued by the photographers. Even during the program's heyday, between 1936 and 1942, its photographers could never quite agree on what *documentary* amounted to or how their pictures of the Depression fit snugly, if at all, with the New Deal programs they were purportedly championing. The FSA's vision of an activist, instrumental, and photography-based archive of social concern was only one of many ambitions for documentary to which the photographers subscribed. They famously fought with Stryker and departed from his shooting scripts. They considered themselves independent contractors who had free rein to cover assignments as they pleased and, in many cases, to submit only a small portion of the shoot. And even for those photographers, such as Russell Lee, who generally accepted the commitments and terms of the FSA, the struggle to provide an honest and immediate representation of contemporary social experience and of the "perennial human spirit" gave rise to alternative and competing ideas for documentary work. What, in fact, was "honest"? Among the vast array of "contemporary social experiences," which might be considered recognizable and legitimate? And how could the camera capture something so evanescent, so extraordinarily complex? Among photographers, the answers to these questions varied greatly.

Coauthored by the literary scholar Sara Blair and the art historian Eric Rosenberg, this volume of the *Defining Moments in American Photography* series offers new ways to understand the work of the famous FSA photographers by exploring an expanded and much more variable idea of the documentary than the one Stryker and the FSA proposed. They follow in the path of scholars who have, on the one hand, looked critically at the FSA photography project and identified its goals, biases, contradictions, and ambivalences and, on the other, discerned strikingly independent directions among its photographers.[6] But what distinguishes this work from that of others is the authors' wrestling with a specific term often applied to the Depression era: *trauma*. If documentary, as a genre, and FSA photographs, as an umbrella project, came to prominence during a time of trauma, and if, in the hands of socially minded photographers, it was meant to address and publicize trauma, the coauthors of this volume seek to understand how trauma and photography mixed and how, in the volatility of that mixture, the competing ideas of documentary took shape.

Trauma is a physical or psychological wounding resulting from a shock or violence to the body or mind. Its effects and manifestations on an individual vary, of course, but in the 1930s there was a widespread belief, especially among photographers, that trauma—the wounding in ordinary people caused by unprecedented deprivation and despair—could be illustrated in pictures. Take one of Dorothea Lange's most famous pictures, *Wife of a Migratory Laborer* (also known as *Woman of the High Plains,* figure 1), showing Nettie Featherston, a hardscrabble farmer living in the dry Texas panhandle, and witness how it matches vividly—photographically—the wounds of Featherston's life story as she told it to the photographer:

We made good money pullin' bolls [cotton], when we could pull. But we've had no work since March. When we miss, we set and eat just the same. The worst thing we did was when we sold the car, but we had to sell it to eat, and now we can't get away from here. We'd like to starve if it hadn't been for what my sister in Enid sent me. When it snowed last April we had to burn beans to keep warm. You can't get no relief here until you've lived here a year. This county's a hard county. They won't help bury you here. If you die, you're dead, that's all.[7]

The ever-present pit of hunger, the fight against the harsh winter cold, the loss of hope, the helpless confrontation with death—the photograph captures a repertoire of gestures and details that suggests the effects of traumatic history and makes hunger and despair visible and iconic: Nettie Featherston's pursed lips, near-crying eyes, hang-dog slouch, nestled forehead, and greasy, unkempt hair.

It was not that Nettie Featherston naturally expressed the blunt force of trauma on her body but rather that the camera was especially good at recognizing or, better, producing it. Simply compare *Wife of a Migratory Laborer* with another, less celebrated picture from the same shoot (*Migratory Laborer's Wife with Three Children [Not in Photo],* figure 2), and recognize in the differences the belief, maybe even the morbid excitement, among photographers and FSA officials, that some pictures, managing the mix of fact and feeling, could make the effects of trauma visible.

In "Against Trauma," Sara Blair takes issue with the commonplace understanding that trauma was a uniquely American phenomenon, defined solely by the Depression as the FSA saw it. So many of the program's documentary photographers were Jews, she reminds us, whose perception of contemporary social experience was shaped by a vivid awareness of other kinds of traumas: the pogroms of Eastern Europe, the Stalinist purges, the Nazi violence. To these documentarians, who in addition to picturing rural poverty also regularly turned their lenses on people living in immigrant and ethnic ghettos and the crowded tenements of the inner city, the very idea of witnessing and picturing social experiences in those places demanded that they come to terms with their differences from "native" Americans of the New Deal and from longstanding histories of representing the city. The first- and second-generation

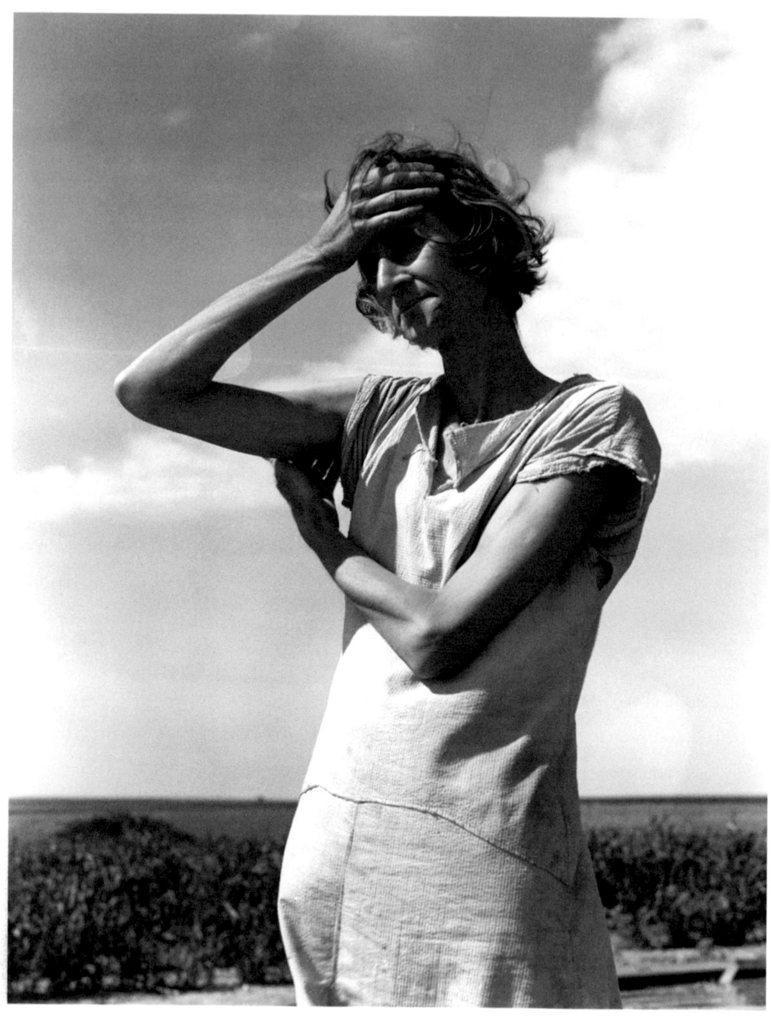

**Figure 1** Dorothea Lange, *Wife of a Migratory Laborer with Three Children, Near Childress, Texas. Nettie Featherston*, 1938. Library of Congress.

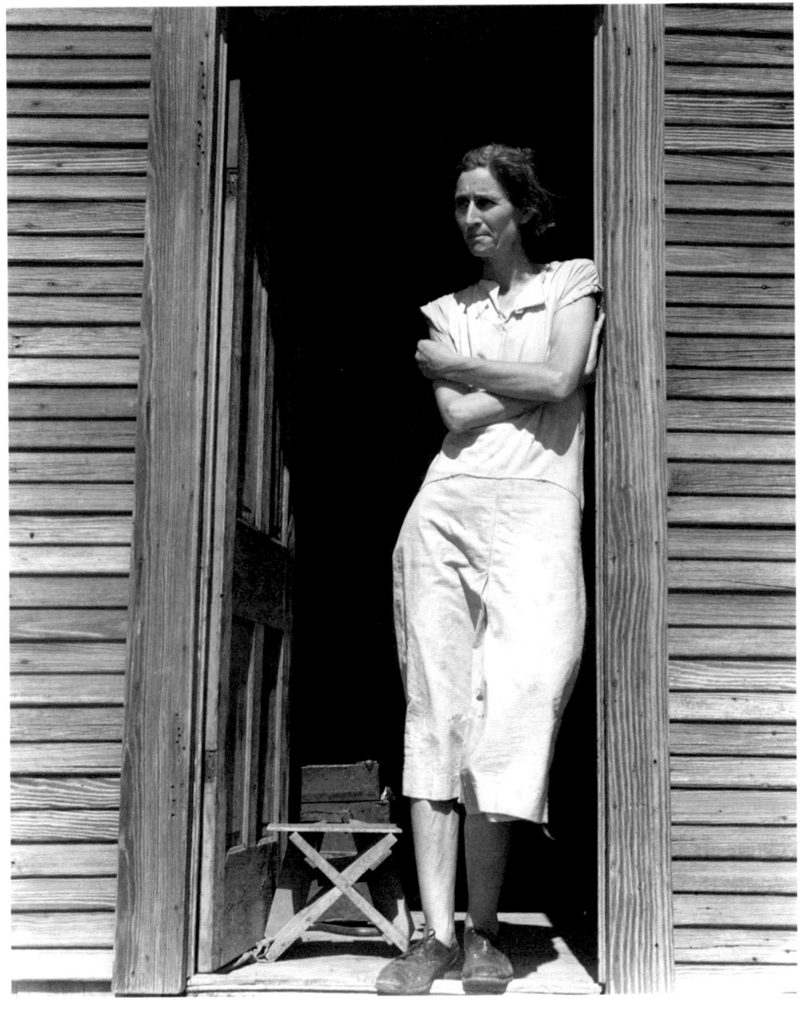

**Figure 2** Dorothea Lange, *Migratory Laborer's Wife with Three Children (Not in Photo). Near Childress, Texas,* 1938. Library of Congress.

Americans on New York's Lower East Side and the African Americans in Harlem, for example, seemed to belong to radically different histories; and in response to that felt truth, documentary photographers found ways to probe the quality and nature of ethnic and racial historical experience, of "historicity" itself, as Blair puts it. She imagines these photographers asking what it meant for Jewish immigrants and African Americans to be not victims, in the FSA sense, but self-conscious dwellers in a different modernity. She suggests how the concerns of a photographer like Ben Shahn were shaped by a wholly different set of terms about historical time and historical experience. In addition, she offers a helpful comparison to the work of the Photo League, a New York–based organization, which offered to FSA photographers like Shahn another model for thinking about an engaged practice.

In "With Trauma," Eric Rosenberg embraces the claim that trauma informed the FSA documentary photographers' practice, but he rejects any simple argument that the photographers merely illustrated trauma or saw it as a repertoire of human gestures, as in Lange's *Wife of a Migratory Laborer*. He suggests instead that the confrontation with trauma warped camera work itself. In his view of documentary, the pain of the world settled not simply in the representation of wounded and injured people but also in the way a picture is conceived and made. That is to say, trauma is not merely an iconography or subject matter—of hungry or homeless people, of the down-and-out, of the ravaged men and women on the farms and breadlines. Rather it is a way of organizing (or not being able to organize) the world through the lens. Or, as he puts it, trauma is a condition so overwhelming that it "denies specialization and deprives one of information, of experience . . . ; it denies documentation." Rosenberg focuses on Walker Evans, the most acclaimed documentary photographer of the era.

To put it simply, Blair argues that some documentary photographers understood trauma in racialized terms and, because of that, understood it as part of a far longer historical trajectory of suffering and discrimination. For photographers like Shahn, trauma during the Great Depression competed with other sorts of ethnic experiences that qualified it and occasionally even paled it. In contrast, Rosenberg argues that trauma was so overwhelming that it was, to a photographer like Evans, almost unrepresentable, at least in any conventional sense. As a writer, Rosenberg confronts the reader with a meditative language and style that also contains eruptions and swift changes of associations, as if enacting a language of trauma itself.

Too much trauma or not enough perspective on it, too overwhelmed by historical conditions or not seeing in it the elements of quiet human struggle—these are among the points of contention in these essays. The authors engage in a generous and lively debate, and together they revise our understanding of the era's most celebrated documentary photography, showing how rich, varied, and contradictory were the projects pursued by the FSA's photographers.

# Against Trauma

*Documentary and Modern Times on the Lower East Side*

Sara Blair

IN THE UNITED STATES, no body of documentary photography has been as iconic as that produced from roughly 1936 to 1940 under the auspices of the Farm Security Administration. The FSA's photographic wing, its Historical Section, undertook to create a record of the devastation that the Great Depression had wrought on ordinary Americans; in offering up an archive of the national trauma, it aimed to convince a national public of the fitness of the New Deal to redress it. In this sense, profound loss was more than just the subject of the Historical Section's unprecedented project: it was its informing ethos. When the archive's mastermind, Roy Emerson Stryker, sent the gifted photographers on his payroll into the field to create "a pictorial encyclopedia" of Depression-era America, his last instructions were: "Keep your eyes open for a rag doll and a corn tester." But by the mid-1930s, this mental map of the United States as a confederation of small merchants and agrarian landholders under threat—"the farms and the little towns and the highways between"—was already anachronistic.[1]

Between 1880 and 1924, the so-called golden age of immigration had created some twenty million new U.S. citizens, preponderantly urban, and the Great Migration of the 1910s and '20s had brought millions of African Americans from the sharecropping South to the industrial Midwest and North. In light of these epochal changes, the project of documenting the ur-realities of rural labor, folkways, and lives was inevitably charged with "nostalgic" feeling—a self-confessed "long[ing] for a time when the world was safer and more peaceful." The "proud land" whose rehabilitation the FSA archive was created to document was increasingly not a matter of land, in Stryker's sense, but of urban and industrial workplaces and dwellings: not the farm but the factory, not the plantation but the tenement, not the lonely byway but the crowded city street.[2]

Of the great wave of New Deal–era documentary photographers, a striking number were individuals shaped by these emerging realities. They were men and women for whom Stryker's defining subject matter and underlying vision of America were decidedly foreign.[3] Themselves not quite American—"sort of foreign born," in the idiom of one of their number—they were recent immigrants or the children of immigrants, overwhelmingly Jewish by origin and culture, and citizens all of that capital of the twentieth century, New York.[4] Intimately familiar with the cultures of the street corner, shop floor, and tenement, they took up the camera not to document a vanishing America but to turn the lens on what they knew—the coalescing lifeworlds of urban work, community, street culture, and struggles to assimilate and survive. Nor did they mourn the memory of a lost American innocence, some "safer, more peaceful" past. Whatever their social status or origins, they owed their own presence in the New World to a succession of definitively modern traumas: pogroms in Eastern Europe, the Soviet revolution, the hard fall of the Ottoman and Austro-Hungarian empires, bloody Stalinist purges, the swift rise of the Third Reich. This shared history attuned them to trauma as the de facto subject of New Deal–shaped documentary, but it also disposed them to resist its assignment to their own experience. Against their framing as victims, history's left behind and dispossessed, they understood themselves as quintessentially modern subjects, attuned to the psychic and temporal dislocations that constituted all social experience in an era of economic stagnation and rapid change.

Some of these photographers, including Arthur Rothstein, Edwin and Louise Rosskam, and Esther Bubley, worked for Stryker en route to careers at emerging journals and media organizations. Others, like Aaron Siskind, Morris Engel, Helen Levitt, and Lisette Model, developed their interests outside the context of the FSA and state-sponsored photography. Whatever their trajectories, many of the most thoughtful documentarians of the New Deal era began or conducted their work in response to a specific site that offered itself up for meditation on the problem of trauma and modern times: Manhattan's Lower East Side. Bounded, more or less, by the East River, Broadway, Canal Street, and 14th Street, the Lower East Side was one of the oldest neighborhoods in New York City, America's original ghetto. Immigrant and working class in character, it had been home to successive waves of Irish, Western and Eastern European, and Asian immigrants, including a high proportion of Eastern European Jews, and its precincts included the sweatshops and garment districts of their fabled labor as well as that legendary street of broken dreams, the Bowery.[5] At least since the mid-nineteenth century, the precinct of the "East Side" had been synonymous with urban poverty and ethnic and racial alterity, and it remained, for uptown New Yorkers (not to mention middle Americans), a world apart, its dwellers seen as dubiously fit for the challenges of American modernity. (In the mid-1920s, when Roy Stryker was a young economics instructor at Columbia University and wanted to expose his well-to-do students to the unchanging facts of poverty and "the slums," the site for his reality missions was none other than the Lower East Side.)[6]

Given this history, dwellers of the downtown streets and tenements were doubly marked by trauma. Victims of poverty and ignorance, they also appeared out of step with the march of progress. In that sense, they were ideal photographic subjects: already "frozen in time," inhabitants of a time that had "becom[e] another place—The Past."[7] Yet the history and experience in the historic ghetto of these Americans in the making bespoke a reorganization of U.S. social institutions and a heterogeneity that was irreversibly transforming the texture of everyday modern life. Their bustling sidewalks, their dingy sweatshops, their crowded theaters and cafés—all were crucibles for new forms of communication, labor, political activity, media, and entertainment that became emblematic of America's modernity even as they shaped it.[8] Both an agency of modern times and an emblem of arrested time, the Lower East Side embodied a condition of strikingly mixed temporality. Worlds away from the sharecropping South and the Dust Bowl West, it was a resonant place to document urgent experiences of American loss and social transformation.

It was also a productive place for meditation on the nature and effects of documentary imaging. To what degree did images of the ravaging effects of the Depression put its subjects beyond the reach of mobility and change, consign them, in the freeze-frame of the photograph, to a superseded order of historical being?[9] Attuned to a legacy of images of the ghetto and its citizens as benighted, atavistic, or unfit for modernity, photographers who experimented with ways of seeing on the Lower East Side made this question central to their practice. In response to the vibrant social life of New York's downtown, they aimed to accomplish something other than the recording of trauma, dispossession, and loss—or even expression of the inevitable failure of such an aim. They sought to remake the photograph itself as a space of experience in which historical being, the urgent problem of belonging in America and to its ever-evolving modernity, could be explored. While the imaging practices of the FSA involved photographic raids on targeted sites of loss and rehabilitation, these photographers' practices were predicated on their shared experiences with their subjects—not least an uncertain or incomplete sense of belonging to interwar America. They wielded the documentary camera not as a power imposed from beyond or above but as an agency activated within vital social relations in service of a social view from below. Their images take on something other than the attempt, as FSA photographer Gordon Parks put it, to "expose the evils of poverty" and bring into view "the people who suffered most under it."[10] At their best, they exploit the temporal structure of photography itself, its agency for arresting time, to address the problem of finding a place in modern times, and they feature the dwellers of New York's iconic downtown as exemplary subjects of that aim. Beyond the project of the Historical Section or the work of exposing social ills, in excess of what we might call the trauma of trauma, these images are interested in what it means to belong to a turbulent history in the making.

To focus on the photographers who made photographic capital of the Lower East Side is inevitably to rethink the aspirations and the afterlives of documentary imaging of the so-called documentary decade. The relevant bodies of work vary widely in aesthetics and reception; their makers shared an animating context and a heightened interest in temporal identity rather than any institutional affiliation. To read their engagements with the social space that was their stage, laboratory, and point of departure requires attention to the social histories of mobility, labor, citizenship, and dwelling that made that space challenging and iconic, and in turn informed the uses of photography as art. What follows, then, is both an argument about the unfolding history of documentary photography in the United States and an attempt to write that history differently, beyond familiar institutional contexts and the familiar art-historical model of the singular, timeless artist. Returning the documentary camera to its embeddedness in a social space marked by temporal multiplicity, we open a new view of its understandings of modern temporality and modern times.

IF THE FSA'S HISTORICAL SECTION has been the paradigmatic institutional context for understanding documentary imaging of the 1930s, we might well take the New York Photo League as its inverse. Re-formed in 1936—the same year in which FSA photographers produced their most storied work, including Dorothea Lange's migrant mother portrait and Walker Evans's images of Hale County, Alabama—the Photo League was a freewheeling photographic cooperative, the offshoot of longstanding Lower East Side traditions of community education, activism, and progressive culture building. Where the FSA was a centralized bureaucracy in service of a state enterprise, the Photo League was a loosely organized group of self-taught amateurs and professionals, collectivist in principle and progressive in outlook, who banded together to share equipment, technical expertise, and ideas (a very wide range of them) about the nature and uses of photography. More to the point, the League's membership was overwhelmingly drawn from the children of Eastern European Jewish immigrants. Its roots in the cultural ferment of the Lower East Side "stamped the League physically and culturally," as one member noted, down to the "grimy stairs" and peeling walls of the walk-up flat in which the group was housed (only visitors were willing "to grab the banister"; the regulars "didn't touch a thing we didn't have to").[11] When the U.S. attorney general Tom Clark included the Photo League on the first blacklist of subversive organizations in 1947, along with the U.S. Communist Party and the Civil Rights Congress, that gesture was conditioned by the group's embeddedness in the culture of the immigrant, working-class Lower East Side.

Yet the work of the Photo League was, at least in its most accomplished projects, far less predictably activist—that is to say, less familiarly documentary—than Clark's judgment might suggest. Consider, for example, one of the earliest images made under the auspices of the Photo League, by the League member (and later storied abstract expressionist) Aaron Siskind, in the tenement apartment of a couple on the Lower East Side (figure 3). At first glance, Siskind's image appears unremarkable. It offers little in the way of visual detail. Its subjects exhibit neither troubling frontality nor evasion of the camera—indeed, they appear to "exhibit" very little at all. But the relative emptiness of the pictorial space and the self-containment of the woman and man are precisely the point, and, for viewers who shared this lifeworld, they would have had clear historical resonance. First, the image recalls a longstanding iconography of the tenements as a site of threatening masses, alterity, and vice, born of a historical moment when the Lower East Side was the most densely populated site on the globe. Indeed, documentary photography in the United States was born on that site: it can be said to have begun when Jacob Riis, a journalist and police reporter turned photographer and Progressive reformer, brought newly invented flash-powder technology into the tenements to expose how America's "other half lives" (figure 4). If Riis aimed to blast the tenements themselves as "hot-beds" of squalor, suffering, and "deadly moral contagion"—at a handsome profit for their absentee owners—his "lightning flashes from the slums" rendered the inhabitants as variously squalid, desperate, and brutalized, and they shaped a national iconography of poverty and the city for a good half century and beyond.[12] Against this foundational archive, Siskind's image insists on what we might call its negative space: the world of experience left invisible, and unimaginable, in earlier documentation of tenement life.

Simultaneously, however, the literal emptiness of Siskind's image speaks to an urgent fact of social life on the Lower East Side: the massive flight of its inhabitants, after two generations of assimilation to American ideals and norms, to the so-called gilded ghettos of the Bronx and Brooklyn. By the mid-1930s, massive infrastructural change set in motion by Riis and other reformers had led to the demolition of thousands of tenement buildings. In 1936, under the federal stimulus of the New Deal, slum clearance on the Lower East Side accelerated so rapidly that the entire area began to look, as one distraught resident put it, "as though a cyclone had struck."[13] State-funded gentrification, making way for high-yield commercial and high-end housing developments, was amounting to a full-scale evacuation of lower Manhattan, centered on what was still remembered as "the historical site of the tenement evil."[14]

In the face of this durable memory and the vast social changes it informed, Siskind's photograph pointedly asks what counts as a visual document of contemporary Lower East Side life. His choice of subjects and composition—the logic of the family portrait; the tight angle and close range that emphasize the limits of the space; the visible evidence of garment work, on which the woman, with her neat dark dress and jaunty haircut, intensely focuses—deliberately recalls iconic images of Jewish "sweaters" in the historic ghetto, packed into their Ludlow and Orchard and Hester Street tenements to do piecework in unending shifts. But Siskind invokes this iconography only to make it irrelevant to apprehension of these subjects, whose space the viewer is asked not to judge but to share. His emphasis has shifted dramatically from the traumatic conditions of tenement life to the condition of dwelling. Foremost is the psychic concentration of the two subjects, who produce not garments or factory

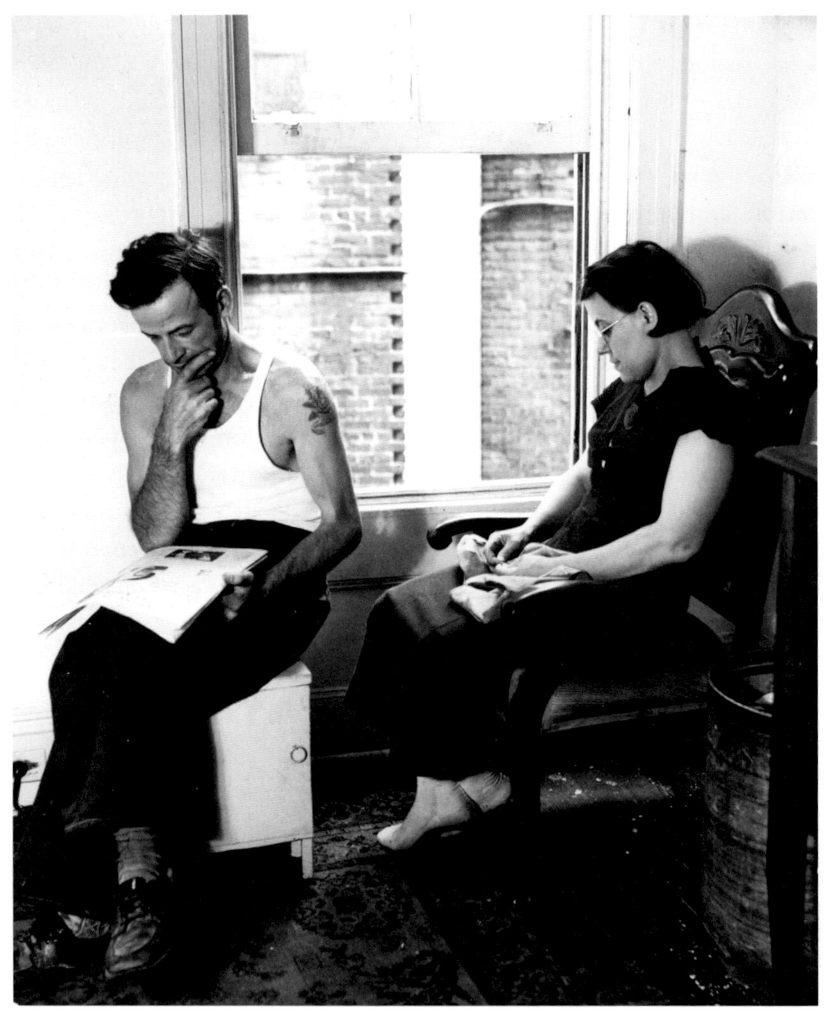

**Figure 3** Aaron Siskind, *Sunday Afternoon: Mr. and Mrs. Joseph Metz* (from "Portrait of a Tenement"), 1936. © Aaron Siskind Foundation, courtesy of George Eastman House, International Museum of Photography and Film.

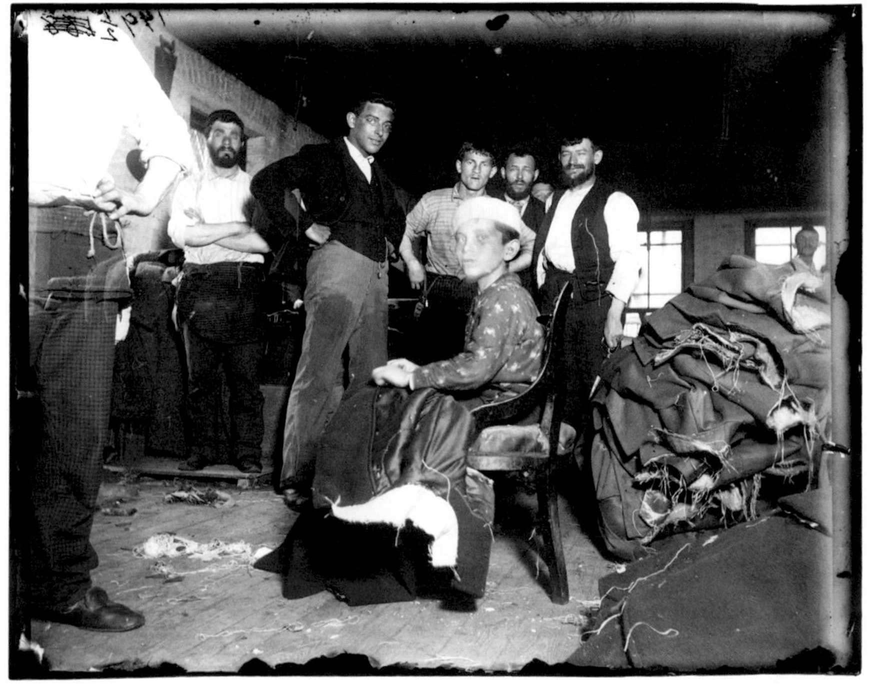

**Figure 4** Jacob Riis, "Twelve-year old boy (who had sworn he was sixteen) pulling threads in a sweatshop," ca. 1899, from *How the Other Half Lives.* Museum of the City of New York.

objects (or for that matter the most obvious product of tenement existence, children) but the lived space they occupy. In stark contrast to the wounded figures whose full-frontal vulnerability characterizes Riis's photographs of the downtown poor (as well as Lange's and Evans's images of sharecroppers and tenant farmers), these tenement subjects recognize no intrusion on their being. They are of necessity aware of the camera's presence, but their stances and affect indicate that it has no power to "take" their images, to drain this place of its made and present meanings for them. Unimaginable as federal rehabilitation clients or Depression victims—foreign, we might say, to these frames of reference—Siskind's subjects feature as individuals who have made a place for themselves in the modern city and in a world defined by dramatic change. His image registers the history of such change, the epochal dispossessions that have brought these subjects and the camera to this place. But the primary effect of the image is to register his subjects' historicity and to leave it undamaged.

Visually unremarkable as it may seem, this portrait of the tenement couple exemplifies the ethos that characterized much Photo League work; it suggests the investment of its members in producing an otherwise timely kind of documentary. Like much League work, Siskind's image was made within a collaborative work unit called the Feature Group, as a contribution to the Group's inaugural project, "Portrait of a Tenement." From the outset, his imagination of tenement life was structured by a tension that would come to define the most self-conscious work of League photographers: the play between familiarity and willed distance. Siskind himself noted that he and his fellow "Tenement" photographers began by "just 'coming on' to the building down the street," moving "up the stairs" to do "a complete study of this little family, three people, sort of foreign born."[15] But this easy intimacy, the nearness of the photographers to their subjects, lends itself not to a predictable affirmation of the "humanity" of the subjects, or of their worthiness for sympathy or social redress. Rather, it encourages meditation on what makes them "sort of foreign" to the camera's eye. Creating a willed distance from known spaces (a distance strengthened by Siskind's use of his favored apparatus, a large-format camera), the "Tenement" portrait emphasizes the way its subjects exceed iconographies of the East Side as well as instrumental modes of documentary encounter.[16] Here, as throughout Siskind's Photo League work, dwellers of the tenements become exemplary American moderns. They are no longer subjects impoverished, left behind, or lost—unless, perhaps, in thought on the felt effects of epochal change or their own assimilation to it. In such Photo League work, documentary imaging functions not mainly as a tool of targeted social reform but as an agency for deeper understanding of the place of everyday subjects in history and in modern times.

This distinctive effect is evident in League members' use of the fabled nitty-gritty of downtown life, its stark materiality and dynamic energies, to create images of striking arrest, in which the usual suspects—tenement dwellers, workers, activists, down-and-outers—figure as subjects caught in the act of confronting their own historicity. Morris Engel's 1937 photograph of a participant in a May Day workers' demonstration (figure 5) gestures toward the urgent social struggles of the moment—the show of force of downtown radical and progressive groups against the effects of the Depression in the city's iconic monument to labor, Union Square—but it renders specific political content illegible. With its tight, dramatic focus, its withholding of visual context that would allow us to see its subject as part of a recognizable collective, it evades both traumatic and heroic rendering of the worker. At stake are not the aims of political movements but the subject's struggle to move at the speed of unfolding history, to take his place within it.

Similarly, Walter Rosenblum's work on Pitt Street, for another Feature Group project focusing on street life on that Lower East Side thoroughfare, features subjects caught in various postures of arrest—most dramatically, a young girl on a swing poised at the very top of its arc (figure 6). Caught at the center of the image, the girl is conspicuously framed by the infrastructure of the historical ghetto—notably the entry ramp onto the Manhattan Bridge, opened in 1909 as part of the infrastructure of exodus, whose effects are registered in the emptiness and protective enclosure of the pictured space. Placed

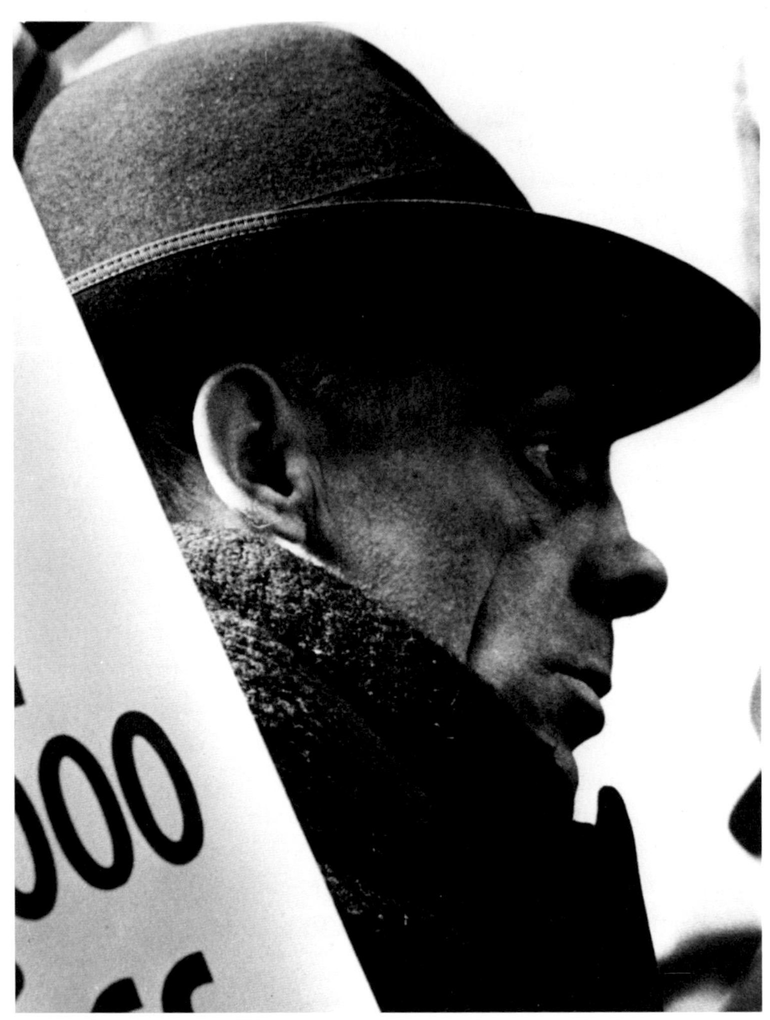

**Figure 5** Morris Engel, *Picket Line, NYC,* 1937, printed ca. 1937. Gelatin silver print, 18 × 23.7 cm. Restricted gift of Phillip and Edith Leonian Foundation, 2011.8, The Art Institute of Chicago. Photography © Art Institute of Chicago.

as she is, the girl is made to embody a decisive tension between the tenement past and the assimilated future, rootedness and arrest, upward mobility and flight, the historicity of the tenement and the progress narrative of modernizing America. Ultimately, the image suggests, that narrative is insufficient to an experiential history that is bound, like the childhood of the girl, to become a past whose usability is powerfully in question.

These kinds of movingly arrested figures recur in early Feature Group projects trained on the iconic spaces of the Lower East Side, particularly in Siskind's archive. A line of anonymous clients at a stand-up lunch counter, visible only from the neck down; a battered man in worn clothes, lost in thought or asleep on a downtown sidewalk beside an outsized machine part whose relation to his immobility is asserted yet made mysterious: all read as deeply inward figures. Their preoccupation with their own presence or capture in the defining spaces of American modernity puts them beyond the reach of state rehabilitation, liberal sympathy, or other mechanisms for addressing traumatic loss.[17] The lone figure who sits in the courtyard of the Catholic Worker Mission, a communal tenement in Chrystie Street housing workers committed to pacifism, social justice, and poverty as a spiritual discipline, embodies this evasion of trauma as a conceptual aim (figure 7).[18] Like his fellow Workers, the subject has embraced dispossession so as to do time in a spiritually meaningful way. His poverty is his wealth, as his withdrawal is his engagement. Caught in meditation, he forces us to confront the insufficiency of conventional documentary knowledge in the face of the mysteries of this way of making time tell.

But Siskind's image isn't straightforwardly affirmative. If its ordered formalism—the strong rectangulars, bold diagonal, and graphic play of light and shadow—honors the sustaining rhythms of social commitment as a discipline, it also troubles the presumption of ready assimilation of the individual to collective discipline. The viewer's eye is led in a measured recessional, from the doorway where the camera arrests itself to the seated man in the foreground to the more distant figure shadowed in the central doorway, and to a third, yet more distant figure behind him. The static quality of the subjects' postures,

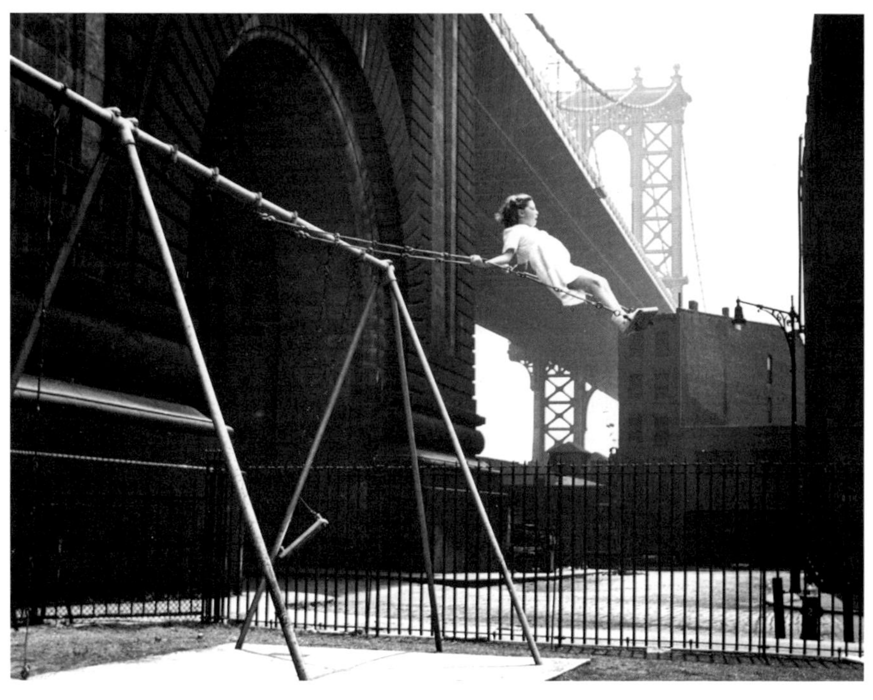

**Figure 6** Walter Rosenblum, *Girl on a Swing,* 1938. Courtesy of the Rosenblum Photography Archive and Howard Greenberg Gallery.

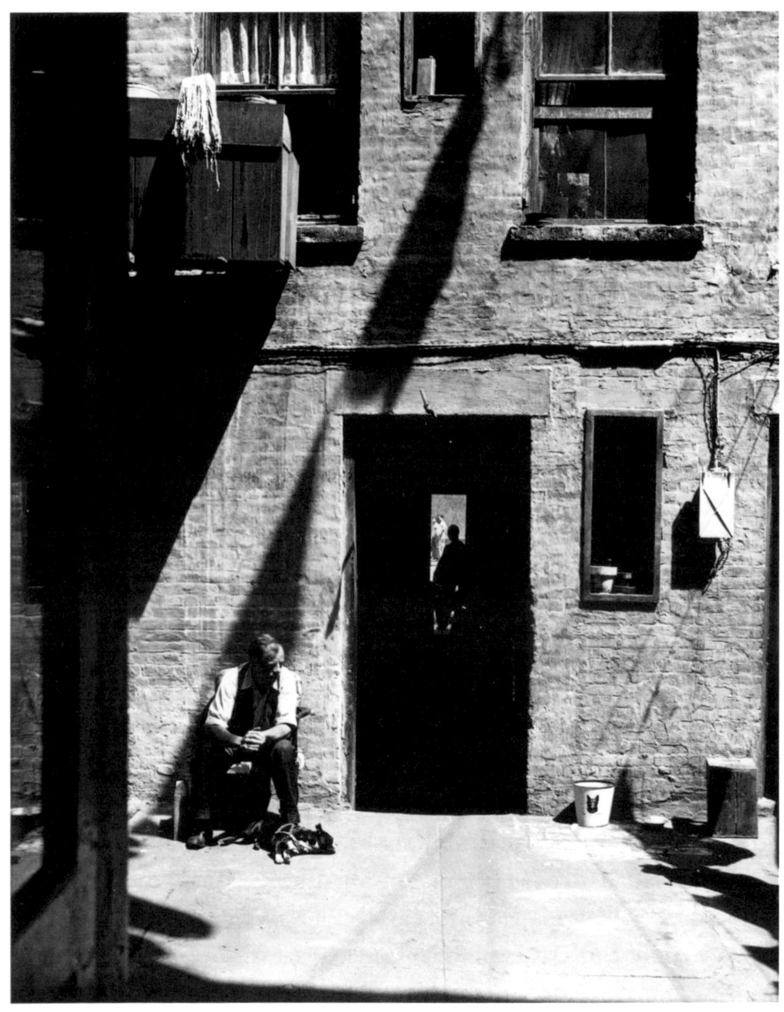

**Figure 7** Aaron Siskind, *Catholic Worker Movement: St. Joseph's House,* ca. 1938. © Aaron Siskind Foundation, courtesy of George Eastman House, International Museum of Photography and Film.

the confusion of inner and outer spaces, the absence of any logic joining these subjects, save their visual arrest—all foreground the problem of naming their social relations. Siskind's photograph offers itself, in other words, not as the record of radical politics or Lower East Side activism, or of a collective forged in the face of dispossession. Ultimately this is a portrait of the tenement dweller as a subject seeking to achieve fuller consciousness about the movements of time and his place within them.

Although Siskind's Feature Group work involved multiple sites and projects, he had an abiding interest in the tenement as a revelatory site for timely meditation.[19] This interest is evident even in his photographs without human subjects. Training his camera on tenement sleeping quarters, narrow staircases, and shadowed hallways, shooting in "sparse" detail, "very simply," "each room at a time," Siskind empties such spaces of visible inhabitants precisely so as to foreground the auratic imprint of lived history.[20] What his camera documents, finally, is the lived being-in-history of individuals, the ways in which they leave the mark of their labor and longings on the lifeworlds they transiently occupy. In a notable image from the Feature Group's project "Dead End: The Bowery," shot in the kind of cheap lodging house iconic to documentary representation of the urban poor, Siskind carefully orchestrates pictorial elements to suggest the power of this space as a site of meditation on dwelling in modernity and time, both for the unseen inhabitant and for the viewer (figure 8). A battered double door, refitted for irregular tenancies, is held precariously shut against intrusion by a small padlock; on the rough flooring beside the entry lies an equally battered box or valise, apparently made of cardboard and gaping in its pronounced emptiness. A mid-thirties icon for those ubiquitous documentary subjects, the down-and-outer and the bindlestiff, the empty carryall has an unsettling effect. It partakes both of the *nature morte*—that centuries-old fine-art genre for raising questions about life and death, permanence and change, and the arresting power of visual technologies—and of the social document, a mode of speaking photographically to the most urgent realities of the present.

As if to emphasize the tension between these temporal frames—the fine

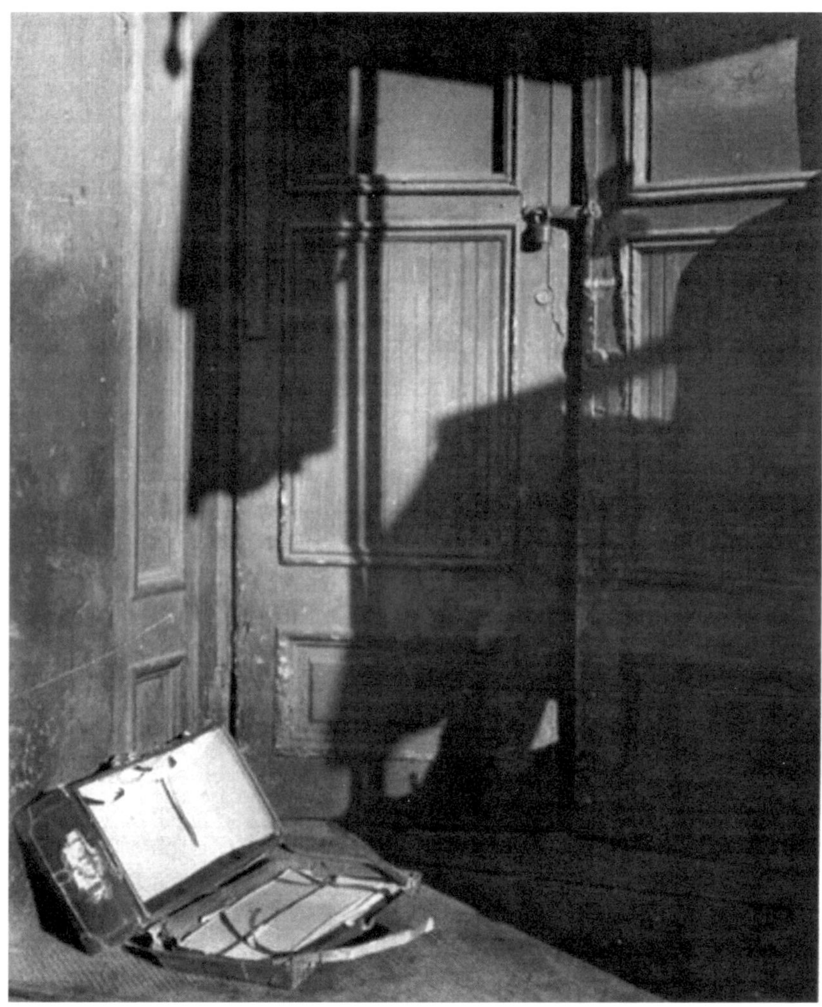

**Figure 8** Aaron Siskind, *Untitled* (from "Dead End: The Bowery"), ca. 1935. © Aaron Siskind Foundation, courtesy of George Eastman House, International Museum of Photography and Film.

art–phenomenological and the documentary-historical—a logic of inversion abounds. Only in the insubstantial shadows that play over the planes of the room do we encounter felt human presence. At the top left of the image, a shadow paradoxically gives substance to the fluid drape of a man's coat or dressing gown; on the right, another communicates the presence of a seated human form. Evacuating the actual Bowery lodger—the archetype of history's refuse, the cast off, used up, and left behind—Siskind frames an existential landscape in which the absent figure regains the power to signify as a representative dweller in American modernity: not victimized, but consciously confronting its facts and its truths. In an important sense, then, the Bowery dweller becomes a surrogate or analogue for the photographer—more specifically, for the documentarian who, as Siskind puts it, eschews "the literal representation" of social damage and loss in favor of "a growing concentration of feeling."[21] This imaginative plenitude depends on the transformation of the iconic density of the Lower East Side as a new density of lived experience. Critically, Siskind grants that plenitude both to the documentary subject or space and to its viewers, thus leveling the relation between them.[22] In this iconographically fraught space, that which is empty—the discarded valise, the room bare of furniture, the negative pictorial space of shadow—testifies to the fullness of lived history; that which has been palpably arrested, caught by the camera, speaks to the fluidity and instability of being in modern time. What better place than the Lower East Side to entertain such paradoxes, to document the lived effects of modernity's storms of progress and change?

Ready to hand as they were on the Lower East Side, the experiential, social, and documentary histories that allowed for such resistance to traumatic reading and for meditation on modernity's times were hardly confined to that site. Indeed, the most storied and widely circulated Feature Group project—the one by which Photo League production has come to be most widely known—wasn't sited on the Lower East Side at all. The Harlem Document, focused on the lifeworlds of the culture capital of African America, involved some dozen Feature Group members working over nearly five years in collaboration with community leaders, cultural institutions, and other partners situated in Harlem; it was the Photo League's answer, in effect, to the Historical Section of the FSA. But even this project (or especially this project) unfolded as an outgrowth of the alternative documentary practices that Siskind, Rosenblum, Engel, and other collaborators developed on their home turf. Alert to the historical links between Jewish and black communities, including the residual life of Harlem as an immigrant Jewish enclave, yet mindful of the structural differences between Jewish and African American struggles for cultural belonging, Siskind cautioned his coworkers that the Harlem Document posed special challenges. In Harlem, he insisted, Feature Group photographers from downtown needed to distance themselves from their lived or acquired "knowledge about the subject," "to become as passive as possible," and at "the crucial moment" of photographic encounter "to permit the subject to speak for itself."[23] What began in Lower East Side streets and tenements as a willed distance from familiar landscapes becomes, in Harlem, an explicit insistence on the limits of documentary knowing and of the camera's entry into living social worlds. In effect, Siskind calls for a heightened arrest at doorways and thresholds, real and symbolic. Only by letting "the facts fall away," he notes, can the photographer meaningfully document other subjects' experience in time—that is, the signal experience for New Deal subjects, particularly African Americans, of responding to the force of their own arrest within rubrics of poverty, dispossession, and trauma.[24]

Siskind's Harlem subjects share with those of the Lower East Side projects an animating self-consciousness about their place in history and in its representations. Framed in Siskind's "very quiet and very formal" documentary mode, they largely evade the sensationalism and condescension of what Roy Stryker called "the goddamn newspaper pictures," the shock journalism and exposé that reveled in poverty, criminality, and a penchant for the primitive as the defining truths of African America.[25] In Siskind's most powerful Harlem Document images, the troubling immobility of black Americans (who dubbed Franklin Roosevelt's policy the Raw Deal for its failure to promote real economic and social equality) enters into the documentary picture not as a condition that can be readily collapsed onto racial "character" but as an experiential fact of modernity, emphasized by the camera.

A resonant example is Siskind's image of a young girl standing beside a dressmaker's dummy in the basement of a Harlem tenement (figure 9). Exploiting the ambiguous effects of the middle distance, Siskind dwells here on the experience of social immobility for his subject. Linked with the dummy—an emblem of her straitened economic prospects, her possible links with craft traditions, her assignment as a modern woman to the role of consumer, and her potential future as a contestant for the attentions of men—the young girl is uncomfortably arrested at the threshold of a troubling sea change. Her posture echoes the stance of an African statuette—it may be an ancestral or art object, a religious icon, a souvenir—carefully placed atop the pile of household goods. This twinning attests both to the radical unevenness of black modernity and to the burden of a collective past whose weight the girl almost appears to shoulder. If she has turned away from the camera toward a space of egress, that space is shadowed and soberingly narrow. In iconographic terms, the way out, up, or beyond the collective past of bondage and failed opportunity remains uncertain.

Even so, the girl's posture bespeaks not victimhood but a willed arrest—a meditative self-consciousness that renders the viewer's sympathy, and even interest, irrelevant. In the end, the young girl figures most powerfully as an individual confronting her place in a history whose lived complexities escape conventional documentary knowing. Like Siskind's Bowery dweller, she figures as an analogue for the photographer and the viewer alike. The image in which she features shares with other Feature Group work a resistance to the rhythms of official documentary imaging—the push and pull of before and after, loss and recompense, trauma and redress. In this sense, Siskind's Harlem documents embody the evolving aims of Photo League work concerned with generating an alternative documentary practice: so much for trauma. In these images, the temporality of arrest associated with the Lower East Side, and with

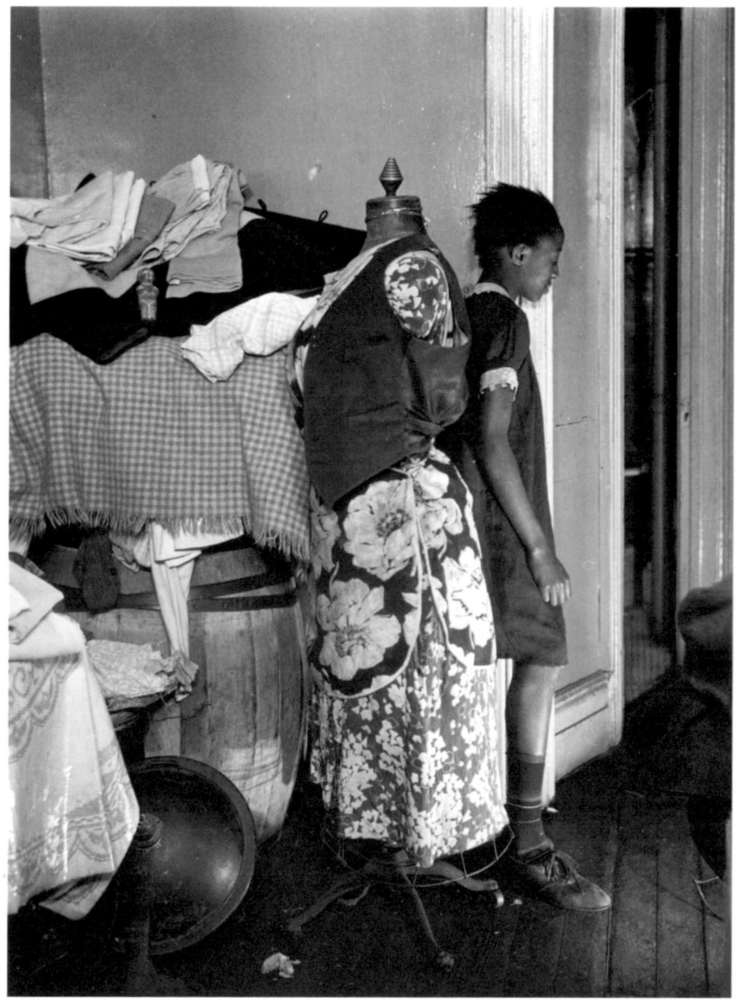

**Figure 9** Aaron Siskind, *Untitled* (from "Harlem Document"), 1932–35. © Aaron Siskind Foundation, Courtesy of George Eastman House, International Museum of Photography and Film.

America's primitives, aliens, and unassimilable others, becomes a resource for meditation on the experience of belonging in history and for challenging widely held assumptions about whose modernity counts. Working in the real time of encounter, Siskind and like-minded Photo Leaguers seize on unutterability and arrest not as the inevitable limit of photography in Depression America but as a condition of possibility for telling a different kind of time.

SPEAKING OF TIME, we might say that the time of photographers like Siskind, Engel, and Rosenblum and of the Photo League has come, as they have begun to attract new kinds of critical attention and to occupy a more visible place in histories of photographic practice. This shift in the record has been accomplished, in part, through an emphasis on specific images or bodies of work that are said to transcend their own status as documentary objects. But the assignment of transcendence comes at a cost, one we can begin to explore by turning to the work of the photographer who is often held up as a model for the production of documentary-era images that break the documentary mold: Walker Evans. In his essay for this volume, Eric Rosenberg argues persuasively for the power with which Evans, the most storied photographer of the New Deal era and perhaps of photo history in general, insists on the impossibility of "giv[ing] voice to trauma in its moment of occurrence." The hallmark feature of Evans's images, Rosenberg suggests, is the felt sense that "some truth central to these photographs is decidedly absent." Evans, in other words, makes images about the trauma of making images of trauma: his photographs inevitably fail to capture that which is their subject, motivation, and aim. Ultimately, however, the absence in question is more than just a conceptual or phenomenological one. From the perspective of the process-oriented, embedded documentary imaging that developed on the Lower East Side, the truth central to the contexts imaged in Evans's photographs—one occluded or rendered invisible, rather than found in its impress or traces—may well be the fact of their subjects' resistance to the rubric of trauma itself. In canonizing Evans's photographs as exemplary instances of, and challenges to, documentary, scholars and curators have tended to accept at face value Evans's suppression of such resistance—or rather, his suppression of the way realities of the "moment of occurrence" enter formatively into his practice.

Consider, for example, the often-reproduced image *License Photo Studio* of 1934 (figure 10). This photograph has a special place in Evans's oeuvre: he chose it as the inaugural image of his landmark 1938 monograph, *American Photographs,* itself a bid, as Allan Sekula puts it, to "reclaim" his work as art (timeless, unbounded by the present) from the documentary agency of the FSA.[26] In an online commentary on *License Photo Studio,* the Metropolitan Museum of Art's photographic curators note that this image "displays Walker Evans's increasingly assured ability to construct meaning out of the juxtaposition" of varying "pictorial elements." The "rebuslike quality" such images achieve, they suggest, is in some way contingent on Evans's interest in "the decaying quarters of New York" City, in particular "the waterfront and the Bowery," but the "battered nobility" he finds there is the product of his distinctive aesthetic vision.[27] Likewise, for the curator Peter Galassi, *License Photo Studio* is emblematic of Evans's interest in photography "as a form of collecting" objects, as well as human subjects, "that struck his eye as signs of the times." Commingling vernacular authenticity with the emerging power of professional advertising, such signage suggests the "inseparability" of sharply divergent practices and temporal modes, and it becomes a favored subject for Evans precisely because it enables him to declare his "equanimity" in the face of commerce, the depredations of progress, and change—"his disinclination either to applaud" them or "to pretend [they do] not exist."[28]

These strong readings (which echo the tenor of received commentary since the initial publication of the image) follow Evans's lead in occluding both the importance to the image of the site he documents and its power to register historicity, loss, and change. *License Photo Studio* was shot in 1934 on Baxter Street, a venue encompassed by New York's historical and iconographic downtown. Four blocks west of that photographic haunt favored by Evans, the Bowery, Baxter Street was not only one of the oldest streets in Manhattan (it was laid

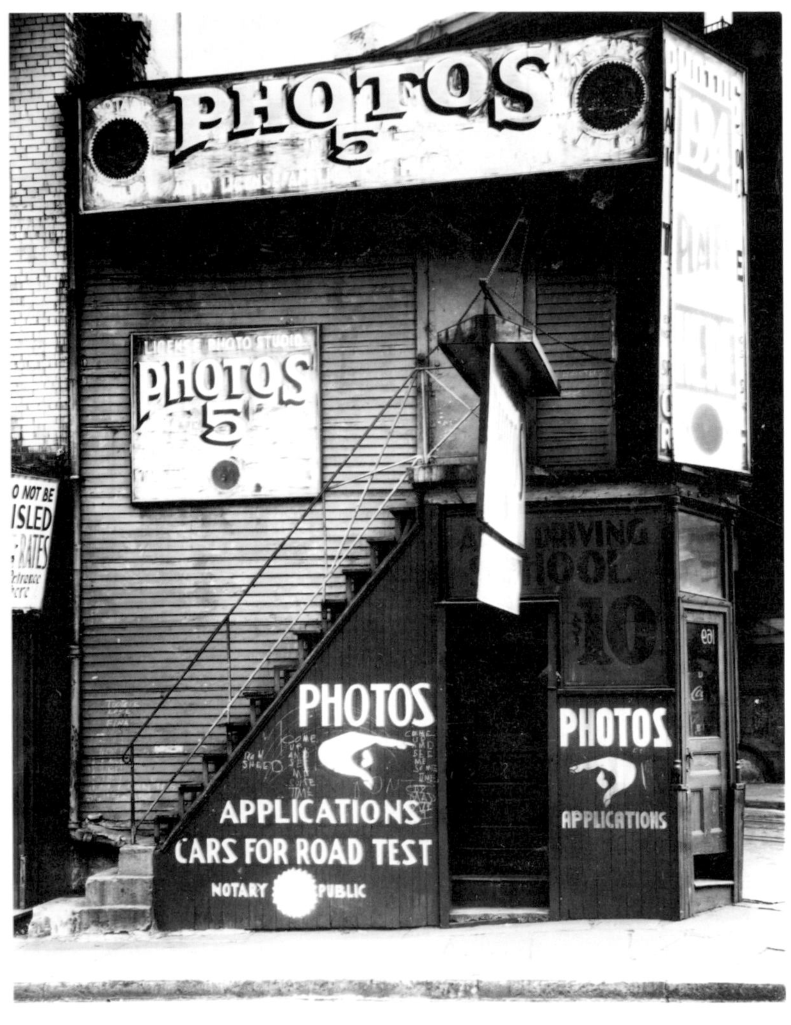


**Figure 10** Walker Evans, *License Photo Studio,* 1934. © Walker Evans Archive, The Metropolitan Museum of Art / Art Resource, NY.

out soon after 1664, when New Amsterdam became New York); it was also the historical epicenter of the slum and tenement problem, with densely concentrated streets making up what had been known throughout the nineteenth century as "the Bend." Jacob Riis, who successfully campaigned to raze the site, called it "the foul core of New York's slums" and made its horrors central to the argument of *How the Other Half Lives,* but his was only one in a long series of outraged screeds.[29] By the mid-nineteenth century, Baxter Street was infamous as the home of the first known opium den in New York as well as of the stirrings of a nascent Jewish garment district; in the earlier years of the century, it was already being called "the most dangerous place in our city."[30] By the 1930s, Baxter Street and its environs had been reformed, rehabilitated, and repurposed within an inch of their collective life, but, like other representative spaces of poverty and failed modernity in downtown New York, it bore the impress of its ongoing social history.

That history haunts, or at least enables, Evans's registration of trauma and his implicit argument about the limits of documentary as its representational technology. In *License Photo Studio,* the profound immobility—what Rosenberg calls the "anarrativity"—of traumatic experience is annexed from the iconic Lower East Side and rendered as the effect of self-conscious documentary imaging—or, more specifically, of a practice that understands the critical difference between "quaint evocation of the past and an open window looking straight down a stack of decades."[31] Yet where does the iconography of downtown leave off and the pictorial logic that marks this image as the work of Walker Evans begin? The relatively small scale of the photo studio structure—a modest two stories, with a rickety external staircase and an irregular footprint, registered by Evans's slight and uncharacteristic deviation from full frontality—suggests its probable earlier life as a jerry-rigged living space or outbuilding, akin to the insidiously "rotten structures" (Riis again) thought to produce Lower East Side subjects wholly unfit for modernity.[32] Pictorially speaking, the relative nearness of Evans's camera has the effect of making invisible that history, in which documentary imaging is so fully implicated. Although a brick structure abutting the studio is visible on the left side of the image, and the hint of another taller building, or at least its chimney, appears along the top edge, Evans's framing cuts this space off from its social context, rendering it visually analogous to the clapboard houses, rural farm stands, and small-town general stores that feature so prominently in his FSA photographs.[33] Thus marooned, the photo studio becomes another exemplary subject for the camera's power to arrest the living present as past—not to register trauma or even its unspeakability, but in effect to create them.

The logic of this transformation becomes clearer when we consider the most striking feature of *License Photo Studio,* the welter of messages affixed to the modest structure—"Photos 5c," "Photos 5c," "Photos, "Applications Cars for Road Test," "Photos," "Notary Public"—interlaced with indexical pointing hands and notary seals (to say nothing of the wry, hand-chalked graffito "Come up and see me sometime"). We might say, after Galassi and the curators of the Metropolitan Museum of Art, that ultimately the subject of this image is the contest of expressive registers—vernacular versus commercial—and the mixed temporalities associated with them—organic or lived and premodern versus machine-driven and progressive. But to assign self-consciousness about the effects of such mixed messages and historicities to Evans's camera, as a distinctive product of his aesthetic, is misleading. At least since the beginning of the twentieth century, writers emerging within the immigrant community on the Lower East Side had begun describing just this phenomenon as definitive of its social landscape. To move through its iconic streets is inevitably, they assert, to engage in precisely such acts of city reading across a welter of Old World and New World signs, of mother tongues and newly acquired ones, of preindustrial and decisively modern vernaculars.

Thus a "green" Jew in Anzia Yezierska's 1928 story "Brothers" notes of the emblazoned streets of the Lower East Side: "I already found out from myself which picture means where the train goes."[34] For the just-off-the-boat protagonist of Abraham Cahan's classic immigrant novel of 1917, *The Rise of David*

*Levinsky,* the first sight of East Broadway, "in the heart of the Jewish East Side," is a streetscape "swarm[ing]" with sign boards, the very icons of "scurry and hustle," in English, Yiddish, and Russian.[35] In Henry Roth's modernist novel of immigrant coming of age on the Lower East Side, *Call It Sleep* (1934), this practice of reading between languages and temporal frames—what we might call reading signs of the intersecting times—has become stylized as a rite of cultural passage. Gazing at the "low sign" of a laundry, "the dull black letters against the dull red," Roth's young protagonist negotiates the boundaries between Chinese, Yiddish, and English, between narrative and iconology, between the arrest of meaning and the temporality of process: "C-h_chuh-Ch-arley. . . . But something else maybe, like Yussie is Joey. . . . Yussie! L-i-ng. Ling. Ling-a-ling. Is Jewish. Can't be."[36] Thus reading, translating, and seeing, the protagonists of these fictions belong to the rapidly changing landscape in a way that, for example, the subject of Evans's *Girl in Fulton Street* does not. Language as an image, set in contending temporal frames and denoting historically divergent social realities, was a signal feature of everyday experience on the ethnic and immigrant Lower East Side.

That East Side citizens were generators and even masters of this welter of temporalities, these signs of the times, rather than immobilized victims of their incommensurability, is asserted in a photograph we can read as an analogue, if not a riposte, to *License Photo Studio.*[37] *Untitled (Sig. Klein Fat Men's Shop, 52 Third Avenue, New York City)* (figure 11) was shot in 1935 or 1936 by Ben Shahn, Evans's friend and studiomate, also a sometime FSA photographer, and himself a first-generation Jewish American. It too features commercial signage and an implied contest of time scales and frames of reference. Yet its interest in loss, historical narrative, and documentary agency diverges sharply from that suggested by *License Photo Studio.* To begin with, Shahn's image is shot not frontally but from an oblique angle, one that mimics, or at least registers, the experience of everyday street-level encounter with urban landscapes by the subjects inhabiting and moving through them. In contrast to the characteristic and deliberate flatness of Evans's image, Shahn's positioning of the camera makes for a certain depth of encounter for the viewer. Within the photographic space, commercial messages are organized in a layered, recessive fashion that mimics classical planar perspective. And if there is no vanishing point into which the downtown streetscape disappears, there is still the beneficent, elevated gaze of the iconic fat man on which the viewer's eye comes to rest.

But Shahn's arrangement of visible elements has more than pictorial effect. The spatial layering of his composition and the implied relation between the viewer and the icon are inextricable from the contending histories and temporal modes embedded in this landscape. Located at 52 Third Avenue, three blocks north of the Bowery above Houston Street, Sig. Klein's indexes a collective migration uptown from the Lower East Side by its growing ranks of "fat men": alrightniks and assimilated Jews who return to the old neighborhood so as to clothe their well-fed bodies with the products of a garment industry that was historically (and, we might say, mythically) the occasion of their rise. Here, too, reiterated text—"Fat Men's Shop," "Fat Men's," "Klein's Fat Man's Shop"—is juxtaposed with iconic images—of the reproduced body of the fat man—in a way that suggests the entanglement in the photograph of signifier, index, and symbol. Shahn, who might be said to have begun his career as a sign painter on Coney Island, shared with Evans an abiding interest in broken, fragmented, and uncommunicative signs, and he plays throughout his work with the peculiar ontology of the photographic sign and its elusive grounds of being.

For Shahn, however, what William Carlos Williams called "the pure products of America" are never the outmoded, vestigial artifacts of a vanished and vanishing past[38]—the peeling minstrel-show poster, the clapboard facade, the rural general store full of parceled and enumerated contents embodying (as Rosenberg puts it in this volume) a "paralysis that can't be escaped." Quite the contrary: it is the metamorphic, dynamic immigrant experience, and even the Jewish and immigrant body, that takes the measure of a rapidly changing lifeworld. Among its commercial promises and entreaties, Sig. Klein dubs itself

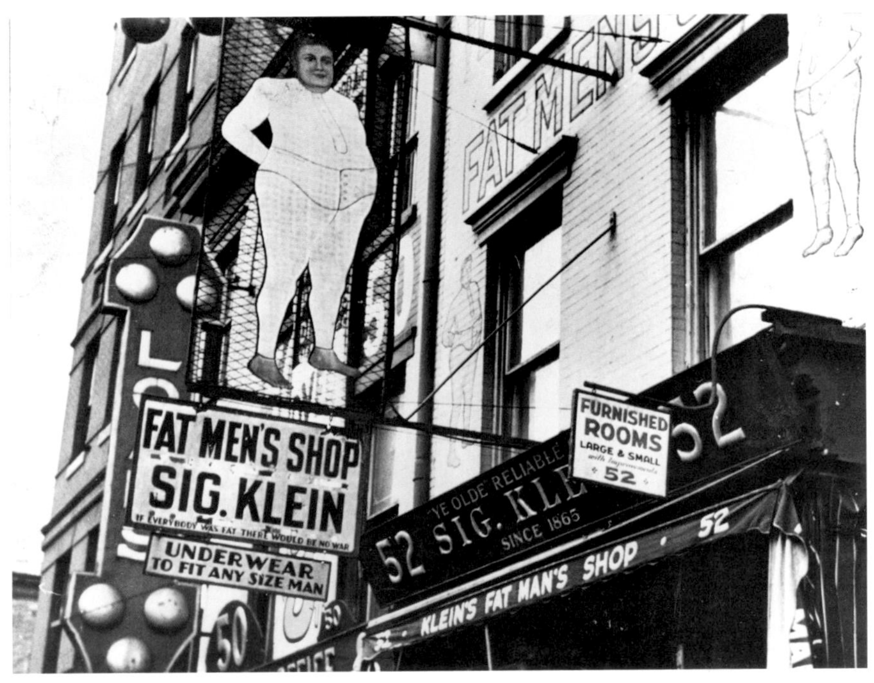


**Figure 11** Ben Shahn, *Untitled (Sig. Klein's Fat Man Shop, 52 Third Avenue, New York City)*, 1932–34. Harvard Art Museums/Fogg Museum, Gift of Bernarda Bryson Shahn. © President and Fellows of Harvard College.

"Ye olde reliable . . . Since 1865." That not insignificant date in U.S. history suggests the storefront's appeal for Shahn (who made numerous photographs there in 1935 and 1936): the stake of its address to East Side passersby in founding narratives of American modernity and the ongoing dream—failed, yet still definitive—of a more perfect union. The past on which America will grow, these signs suggest, is not that of the Anglocentric inheritance gently mocked by their commercial diction, but the alternative past of immigrant and ethnic striving, which produces subjects and citizens fully capable of meeting modernity's challenges ("Underwear to fit any size man"; "Furnished rooms large and small"). In the rhetoric of wish fulfillment, this is a foundation for the future in which victimhood and the underclass have been left decisively behind: "If everybody was fat there would be no war."

Shahn's photograph underscores the self-mocking quality of this rhetoric and its foundational investment in the assimilation model, implanted, by the mid-1930s, in the heart of Jewish American (as well as unhyphenated American) culture. In 1936, the radio comedy *The Rise of the Goldbergs,* featuring a working-class Jewish tenement family, went into national syndication on the strength of its focus on ethnic striving for social security and the intergenerational struggles of immigrant family life. Having found a new home on the NBC network, it would soon move its own protagonists to the suburbs and begin chronicling their assimilation to middle-class norms. (One community educator of the era claimed that the series, with its emphasis on Jews as good Americans and good neighbors, "has done more to *set us Jews right* with the 'goyim' than all the sermons ever preached by the Rabbis.")[39] Among former citizens of the tenements newly resident in the gilded ghettos, concern was stirring about the psychic and existential costs of economic success. If the Depression dramatically worsened the living conditions of the most vulnerable Lower East Siders, the more pervasive threat or loss defining the collective social experience of this era turns out to have been what the historian Hasia Diner calls the "surrender of Jewishness for America."[40]

The signscape of Sig. Klein's clearly registers this labile mid-1930s context of assimilation, invention of the past, and dynamic change. Documenting its response as such, Shahn's photograph participates in a historically urgent conversation about mobility and immobility, loss and reanimation, uncertain futures and usable pasts. This is hardly the insistence on modernity as trauma and damage spelled out—literally—in Evans's *Truck and Sign* or on the camera as a time machine for imagining "what any present time will look like as the past," as in Evans's *License Photo Studio.*[41] If, as Rosenberg argues, Evans ultimately implies the impossibility of documentary representation in a context of traumatic history, we might say that Shahn is interested in resisting the categorical assignment of trauma as fate to the men and women who people his images, the subjects both of camera work and of American modernity. In Shahn's practice, particularly the aspects of it shaped directly by his identification with the Lower East Side, the documentary camera becomes a means for exploring uneven, not arrested, development: the lived effects of intersecting histories and uneven temporalities. And these effects, Shahn implies, define not only life on the Lower East Side but social being itself in New Dealt, downsized, restructuring America.

Shahn is a useful figure for triangulating the documentary practices of Siskind and the New York Photo League on the one hand and Evans on the other, and thereby reconsidering the effects of documentary practice during the documentary decade. Like Siskind, Shahn was the son of Eastern European Jewish immigrants, raised in the Jewish enclave of Williamsburg in Brooklyn. As a youth he apprenticed as a lithographer and printmaker on the Lower East Side and came of artistic and political age there. Its cultures of activism, leftist expression, and public arts were both the vehicle and the subject of his most storied work as a painter, graphic artist, and illustrator.[42] Like Evans, with whom he shared a studio and living space intermittently during the early 1930s and from whom he received his one and only lesson in the uses of the camera ("f/9 on the sunny side of the street, f/4.5 on the shady side of the street. For a twentieth of a second hold your camera steady"), Shahn was an employee of Roy Stryker.[43] But he served the U.S. government as a member of the FSA's Special Skills unit, charged with creating graphics and visuals in support of agency programs, rather than the Historical Division. This gave him unusual freedom to choose and pursue his photographic subjects and to evade some of the most constraining features of FSA-sponsored documentary.[44] Conceptually, his irregular status enabled him to reimagine the work of documentation as a complex play between the arresting image and the human histories that brought its subjects to the place and state registered by the camera. As part of a Stryker-led project titled *Ohio Harvest,* shot in 1938, Shahn was asked to visit FSA resettlement communities, whose "neat little rows of houses" he found it "impossible to photograph." In lieu of evidence of the ordered regularity of state-managed lives rescued from poverty and oppression, Shahn sought out the lived, auratic landscapes being made redundant and invisible: "Where . . . they br[ought] you from," where these lives "began." For Shahn, each documentary engagement involved a narrative logic, but not exactly the kind imposed by the standard editorial photo story or by Stryker's famously directive shooting scripts ("Keep your eyes open for a rag doll"). What Shahn sought was a dialectic between motion and arrest, an embedding of his subjects in experience, change, and time: "Almost like a movie script except [the images] were stills."[45]

A tension between still and mobile images not only animates Shahn's documentary series production but also governs the pictorial structure of his most ambitious photographs and ultimately distinguishes his interest in temporal challenge, change, and arrest. In his work for the FSA, Shahn produced photographs of sharecroppers, rural laborers, and crowds at patent-medicine shows whose subjects occupy these contexts in a way that suggests temporal simultaneity and spatial discontinuity. The effect, as the photo historian Nicholas Natanson notes of Shahn's images of plantation labor in Pulaski County, Arkansas, is of subjects "*alone* together," caught at the same instant in radically different modes of inhabiting the same social world.[46] That effect inverts the force of Shahn's photographic forays on the Lower East Side, which typically imply spatial coherence or unity—a shared site of experience—and temporal multiplicity: divergent ways of being in time. Along these lines, we might consider Shahn's image of a South Street pier, shot between 1932 and 1935 (figure 12). In its composition and framing, this image insists on the collective identity of its four subjects, tightly organized around the central vertical axis and bound by the visual rhythm of their headgear, the white collars, kerchief, and cap, and the rounded forms of their heads playing against the stark rectangularity of the frame. Apparently unaware of the camera—Shahn may already have put to use the right-angle viewfinder that allowed him to make images by stealth, without his subjects' knowledge—they appear arrested in varying postures: anticipation, exhaustion, boredom, reverie. Yet the image they inhabit is far from static. The dramatic tilt of the camera, echoing the motion of swelling waves, and the nervous play of ropes and cables leading the eye upward toward a point of convergence far above the horizontal edge convey an experiential mobility and dynamism toward which the photographic record can only gesture.

Even more powerfully, the relation of spatial and temporal modes in the image bespeaks Shahn's interest in layered and contending historicities. In tension with the tightness of the figural grouping, the notable variety in the clothing and stances of the subjects emphasizes social disjunction. Collectively, they form something like a visual equivalent of the familiar nursery rhyme: "Rich man, poor man, beggar man, thief." More to the point, these figures seem to belong to distinctive—if not radically different, or even incommensurable—historical contexts of Depression, mobilization, modernity, and assimilation. What makes the image arresting, photographically speaking, is the simultaneity of these temporal frames within the photographic field. By what pictorial or social logic are the active sailor, the four-in-hand dandy, the faceless, apparently weathered figure of exhaustion, and the traditional immigrant woman, with her headscarf or *sheytel,* bound together?

Shahn's handling of the background and implied context of the photograph

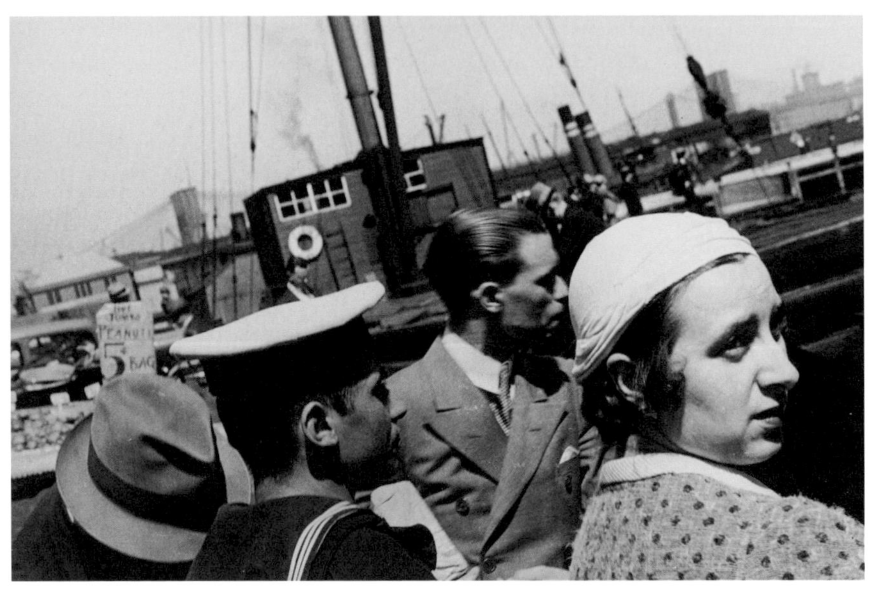


**Figure 12** Ben Shan, *Untitled (South Street pier, New York City)*, 1932–34. Harvard Art Museums / Fogg Museum, Gift of Bernarda Bryson Shahn. © President and Fellows of Harvard College.

provide a critical clue. Skimming the horizon line in the distance, deliberately demoted from the iconic status conferred upon it by photographic modernism and myths of assimilation, the Brooklyn Bridge anchors the photograph's treatment of its temporally coded subjects. Nowhere in evidence is the bridge's power as a symbol, since its opening in 1883, of American technological mastery. Rather, the exaggerated span of the bridge across the extended diagonal emphasizes its function in the Depression context as a bridge to nowhere.[47] From this vantage point, from the piers facing northeast, neither the approach to the bridge, along Dover Street south of the Bowery in Manhattan, nor its terminus in Brooklyn is visible. In this respect, too, Shahn undercuts a historically urgent iconography of immigrant mobility. In composition, subject matter, pictorial logic, and scale, his photograph activates the image of upward and outward mobility only to trouble its underlying premises. The four subjects pictured on the pier, or perhaps in the stern of an approaching ferry, embody the sustained power of myths of arrival to the New World in shifting historical frames. Collectively they recall, as they suspend, myths of arrival and belonging, of the many as the one, of huddled masses transformed into modern citizens. Yet, framed as they are, these subjects can hardly be assimilated to any unified narrative of progress or modernization. Nor are they readily cast either as victims or victors in an instrumental narrative about the modern state as an agent of progress. Their unfixed status is heightened by the shifting status of this photograph as a document, which captures but also creates the effect of temporal multiplicity. Finding and composing this social landscape, Shahn's image implicitly argues for the distinctive power of the documentary camera to offer up lived, historically urgent paradoxes of mobility and immobility, of dramatic arrest and change.

Such temporal unmooring, with its implication of broader views of American progress and social being in modernity, becomes a powerful feature of Shahn's work on the Lower East Side. In his downtown portfolio, the tension he identifies between "movie" sequencing and "stills" is generative and structural. A striking number of these images are composed so as to create a visual experience of serial rather than conventionally multiple human subjects, who have the effect of inhabiting varied, even competing temporal frames in a single landscape or space. In one untitled shot, three dark-clad, elderly men stand in front of an advertisement for women's undergarments (figure 13). If the truncated messages— "—rsets," "—s—ier—s"—don't quite "stutter," as Rosenberg suggests of Evans's signage, their instrumental function has been sharply undercut by the positions of the foregrounded figures. The point of the image is not some kind of commentary on the labor of these men, on the disjunction between the advertised goods (feminine unmentionables) and their sartorial sobriety, or even on the waywardness or mystery of signs. Rather, the photograph bespeaks a by-now familiar temporal multiplicity and disjuncture. Although the two men on the right touch—their bodies become virtually indistinguishable—their gazes and stances, their modes of self-presentation, mark them as belonging to different orders of being in modernity and in Jewish American history.

In particular, the men's hats, rhyming objects across the visual field, imply notably different historicities. The man on the right, his heavily lidded eyes almost closed, wears a generous beard and a black wool fedora of the sort associated with transplanted Orthodox culture. Thus arrayed, he might well be a figure of prayer in a sacred Jewish context. The subject in the middle of the trio and the image wears a light gray hat, perhaps also felt or wool but sporting a wide black ribbon. His gaze, available though shaded, and his closely trimmed beard place him in a different temporal regime, that of an ambiguous secularity and assimilation. The figure at the left, separated from his fellow Lower East Siders by a small gap as well as a posture that breaks the visual rhythm, moves further still along the implied historical continuum. With his jaunty, fashionable white panama hat and his clean-shaven chin, with the glossy sheen of his neatly knotted tie and the starched precision of his dress collar, this subject bespeaks full belonging to the order of secular urban modernity. Against the inward gaze of the black hat and the wary gaze of the middleman, his gaze alone asserts a power to examine their shared lifeworld and to judge or scrutinize

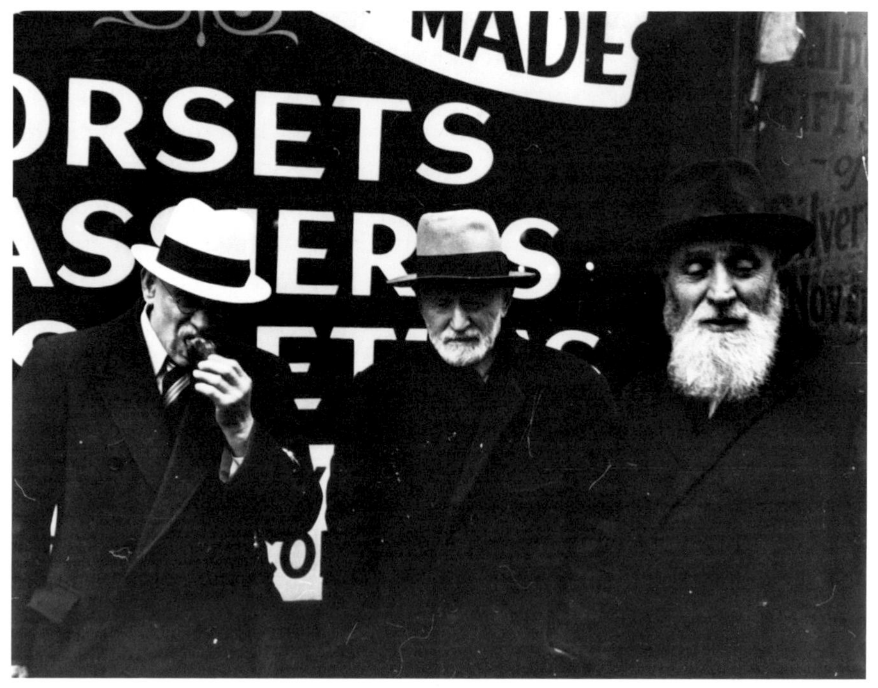


**Figure 13** Ben Shahn, *Untitled (Lower East Side, New York City)*, 1936. Harvard Art Museums / Fogg Museum, Gift of Bernarda Bryson Shahn. © President and Fellows of Harvard College.

the goods it puts on offer, its old and its brand-new articles of faith. As composed by Shahn, these figures suggest neither the arrested development long associated with the Jewish ghetto nor a mode of reverie conditioned on pastness, as in Evans's work, but a space of experience in which competing frames of historical reference are simultaneously in play.

That Shahn self-consciously seeks to produce such simultaneity is confirmed by the uncertainty here of the viewer's visual orientation and what that uncertainty implies about how to understand the temporality of modernity. Himself a native speaker and lifelong reader of Yiddish, Shahn often made reverse prints or painted images of his negatives, experimenting with the shifting effects of a left-to-right orientation (as in English-language reading) versus the right-to-left movement of Yiddish and Hebrew texts. Intrinsic to the composition and rhetoric of mobility and stillness in Shahn's East Side is an ambiguity about which of these orientations applies, and with what effects. The dominant narrative of interwar Jewish America—that of unimpeded assimilation and access to cultural citizenship—would dictate a triumphalist reading of Shahn's subjects, framing them as exemplars in a willed progression from traditional Judaic subjectivity to the figure of the alrightnik, wholly self-possessed in the secular metropolis. Ironically, of course, this reading depends on the viewer's adoption of a Yiddish (or culturally Jewish) orientation, reading from right to left. Furthermore, the dynamics of the image resist such easy historicism; they send the viewer's eye back to the Judaic figure, whose very unavailability or inwardness resonates as a meaningful response to the unstable temporality of the Lower East Side and of the American modernity it shaped and has been made, iconographically, to oppose. In a further irony, the reader experiences this revisionary relationship to Old World Judaism only through an English-language (or American) orientation, moving from left to right. What, after all, is being documented here? The hard social facts, the upheavals in history that bring these figures together in this time and in this place may remain invisible to us. The point of the photograph is to bring home the challenge of accounting for our own place in this fugitive temporality. How does the viewer *look*, in the face of such subjects who are uniquely fit to embody the challenge of telling modern time?

LIKE SISKIND'S USE OF ARREST, Shahn's interest in still yet moving images bespeaks a rejection of the rubric of trauma both as the defining subject of documentary (what Eric Rosenberg calls its "engine") and as the ground of being of the photograph. In response to the conditions of being (rather than those of living) on the Lower East Side, photographers in its ambit had no ambition to see the present as always already past, as Evans did: to make souvenirs against the traumas of dispossession and vanishing. Rather, they aimed to create images in which multiple historicities, multiple temporalities, are made simultaneously available and urgent for the viewer. If their images are signs of the times, it is not "anarrativity" that characterizes them but the uneven effects of translation. Likewise, these alternative documentary images have no aspiration to transcend their subjects or the conditions of their own coming into being. Their rootedness in the wayward temporality of immigrant, exile America, as in its iconic space of motion and arrest, is intrinsic to their implied claims for what it means to document the experience of modernity. This renewed, or perhaps updated, commitment to the mixed temporality of the photograph would become generative for photography—their own and that of other artists—of the postwar era. Already in Siskind's downtown work, we can see the emergence of the interest in mark making as marking time that would shape his influential abstract expressionist images of the 1950s and '60s; in Shahn's, we see the transformation of the subjects of socially conscious imaging as the figures of introspection, fugitive historicity, and reverie that would characterize so much of the practice of postwar street photography and subjective documentary.

That such photographic futures are already imaginable in the imaged present of Shahn's work is evident in another Lower East Side photograph (figure 14). In *Untitled, Lower East Side* (April 1936), Shahn offers the viewer a meditation on the structural paradoxes of a historical being experienced in

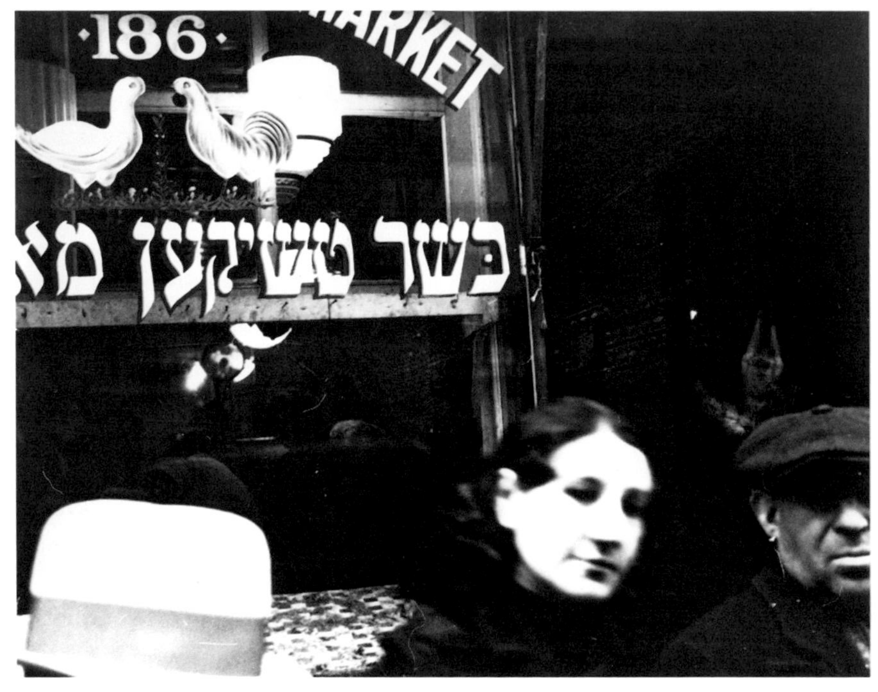


**Figure 14** Ben Shahn, *Untitled (Lower East Side, New York)*, 1936. Harvard Art Museums/Fogg Museum, Gift of Bernarda Bryson Shahn. © President and Fellows of Harvard College.

tension with its received iconography, and those of documenting the effects of temporal arrest. Shot outside the storefront of one of the kosher butchers whose presence indicated the survival of traditional Judaism, his three subjects pose not only alternative modes of inhabiting American modernity but also competing aesthetics aligned with them. The figure on the right of the image, partially cropped, eyes shadowed beneath the bill of his workman's cap, suggests the mute stolidity of the ethnographic subjects of Jacob Riis, caught by the lightning flash of the camera and denied the power of a returning gaze. The figure to the left, reduced to his jaunty white hat, becomes a mere compositional element; he is the embodiment of an instrumental modernity embraced by photographic modernism and Sig. Klein's Fat Man alike. Mediating their relation is the slightly out-of-focus figure of the young woman: dreamy, evocative, intensely private. Neither ethnographic certitude nor the ordering powers of formalism can do justice to her historicity. Exceeding them, she generates the felt requirements for an alternative way of seeing. That this perspective must be temporally mixed, counter to Evans's view of "time present as time past," is confirmed by the paradoxical sign of the times that embellishes the darkened storefront. Its emblazoning reads, in transliterated Yiddish, "*Kosher tshicken ma[rket].*" Whose history is reflecting, or reflecting on whom? To what degree does experience on the Lower East Side already refract American modernity in ways that remain invisible to "native," English-speaking Americans? Trauma, what lies outside the frame, is beside the point. Already the young woman looks forward to a photographic future in which psychic distance and temporal arrest have become key to documenting states of experience, mind, and being. Still moving, in place, with a historicity that exceeds the fixed forms of history, she mirrors the viewer's own condition of unstable belonging; she intensifies the irreducible power of realities found and confronted, rather than wholly invented or made. In such an image, in this place, photography is transforming itself before our very eyes as it looks to a postdocumentary future by repurposing an iconographic past.

# With Trauma

*Walker Evans and the Failure to Document*

---

Eric Rosenberg

TRAUMA AND DOCUMENTATION WOULD SEEM to be mutually exclusive. The one is elusive, invisible; the other is all presence and proof. Both represent conditions of totality, of essence. They describe modes of being seemingly complete in and of themselves. Photography in the United States in the 1930s demands time and again that such antithetical conditions be productive. Trauma was the subject of photography in this moment. Documentary style, what Walker Evans would come to claim as his practice, was trauma's vehicle.

The practice of photography in the United States during the Great Depression was in part dependent on these mutually exclusive conditions. Their entwining was the engine driving the possibility of photography. Though Evans's work seems at times only to come to this relationship between document and trauma with the employment provided by the Farm Security Administration and his attendant dispatch to Alabama in 1936, in fact the immeasurable distance between and startling proximity of trauma and documentary are evident almost from the outset of his photographic career.[1]

*Luna Park Sign, Coney Island* (figure 15) of 1928–1929 is commonly taken as evidence of an interest in abstraction following from the photographer's return from Paris in 1927—a sympathy for modernist languages of painting, for photography's having to take its place in a world of practices with predetermined modes of expression. These traits would be evacuated from Evans's work by the mid-1930s but make all the sense in the world around 1927–29, in the midst of American transatlantic culture and up to the edge of the Depression.[2] The image seems all cubist, an exercise in formalism. Disintegration and destruction, as conditions of material surroundings, as subject, as inherently embedded in those formations of meaning, seem impossible. At the same time, something about the world as incomplete, as defined as much by loss and absence of coordinates and comfort seems implied here, something Evans is perhaps struggling to literalize.

By 1930 Evans had made plain his convictions, or at least those expressed by his work to that date, as to the component parts of the intersection of trauma and document, their inevitable meeting and the necessary belief in the impossibility of their association, the extent to which the very fact of one might spell the negation of the other.[3] *Truck and Sign* (figure 16) is a deceptively simple image of two men handling a large, electrically illuminated sign spelling the word "Damaged." It is unclear whether the pictured laborers are moving from right to left or left to right and whether they are loading or unloading the sign. Other marks of a destabilizing sense of environment are evident. The sign is enormous: it surely will be (or was) mounted quite high and would command a broad swath of vision. It dwarfs both its handlers and the truck. But because the truck must be nearly as long as the sign itself, we can infer that most of the vehicle is outside the right-hand edge of the photograph. As a result, the truck's uncanny foreshortening is deeply disturbing in relation to the full expanse of the sign itself. How could such a vehicle convey such an object? Damage as a condition of visual understanding is made to characterize the reality offered by the photographic image. And that reality is closed and total: the truck belongs, after all, to the Globe Elec. Sign Co. The whole of a world is implicated in the set of unfathomable relations described by the action and circumference of the photograph. Moreover, the cropping out of the truck leaves crippled the part that is visible. In its current state—its state as ruin—it can hardly appear to support the product it purports to carry. A failed economy of deliverance is the result; a job is lost.

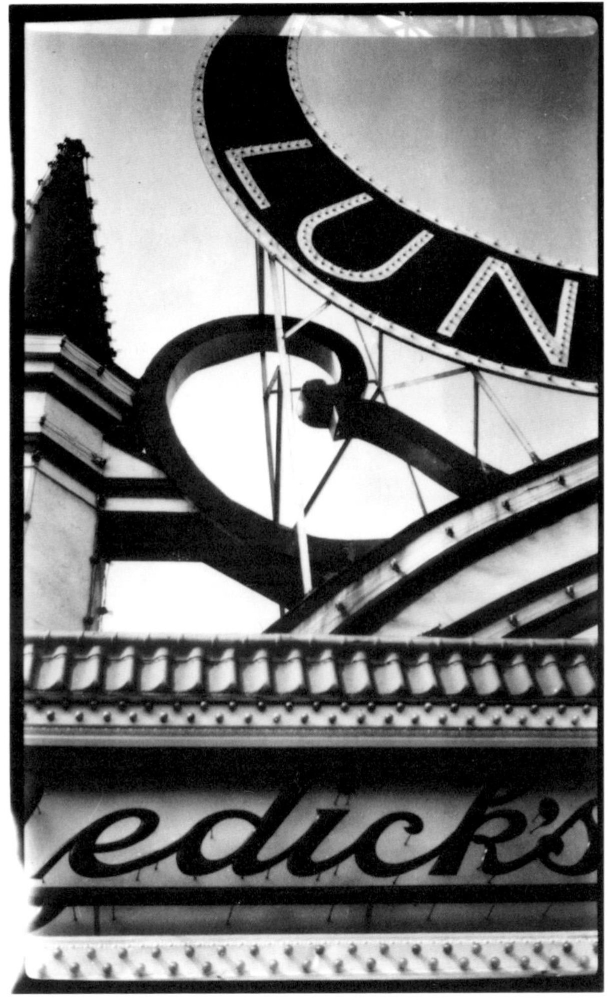


**Figure 15** Walker Evans, *Luna Park Sign, Coney Island*, 1928–29. © Walker Evans Archive, The Metropolitan Museum of Art / Art Resource, NY.

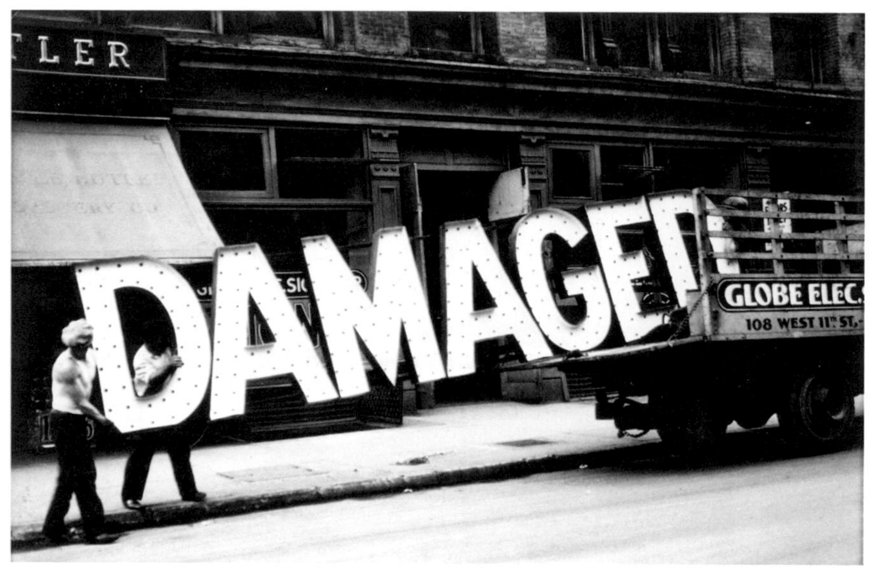


**Figure 16** Walker Evans, *Truck and Sign*, 1930. Gelatin silver print, 8 × 12¼ inches, Collection Miami Art Museum, promised gift of Charles Cowles. Copyright: Provided by Art Resource.

As the human situation attending the scene is rendered visually damaged, so further confirmation of that is offered by the viewer's effort to read as completely as possible, to find in the completion of reading some remedy to the illness or damage made metaphor therein. The workmen perform their task under the incomplete name or word above their heads, which in turn completes a store sign whose last four letters are *tler.* We cannot complete the word. An impulse to find the solution to the puzzle occasions the sounding out of these letters, and in that experience the word *tiller* may be formed in consciousness. All of a sudden the viewer is in the presence of that device already destabilized in the uncanny relationship between men, sign, and truck. Whose hand is on the tiller? Is anyone's? Can the tiller be anything but an incomplete collection of letters failing to spell out meaning, whatever the degree of recognition that might be superficially accorded the term and its possibility?

If the recognition of an allegory of the Depression is unavoidable in the primary motif of the photograph—the "Damaged" sign—coming as it does in 1930, the first full year of the economic collapse that would dominate American life for the next decade, the insistence on lack of control of means, a leitmotif of the photograph's component parts, drives home the allegory of damage.[4] And once the interpretive implications of such a set of relations becomes apparent, it is difficult not to see this drama played out in almost every aspect of the picture. Take, for example, the harsh contrast of light and dark in the juxtaposition of the sign and the storefronts. The dark recesses of the windows and entryway assume a cast of impenetrability as well as immeasurable depth against the glare of the gargantuan letters. It is as if a narrative drama has been added to the street in front of Edward Hopper's *Early Sunday Morning* (figure 17), painted in the same year *Truck and Sign* was made. This is not to argue for a painterly aspect to Evans's photography but rather to say that if we imagine a shared sensibility toward the representation of the Depression, its documentation in some form or another, we also must acknowledge the particularity of Evans's version.

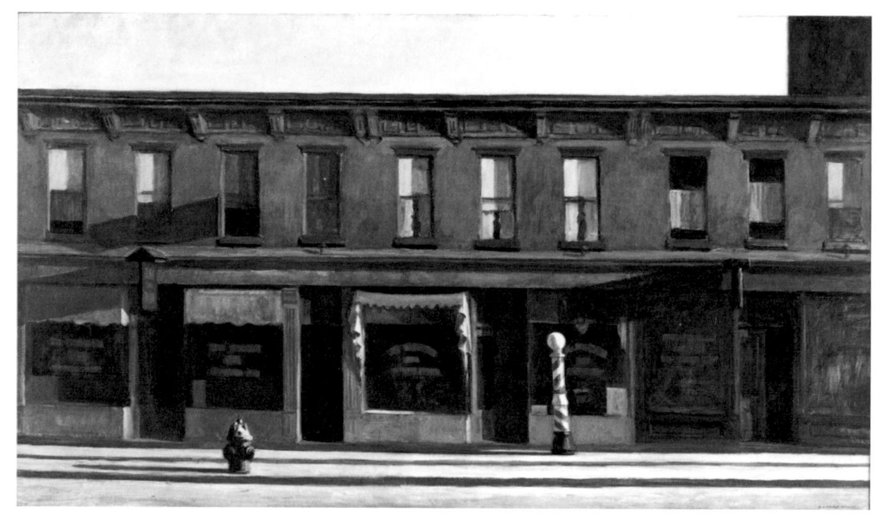

**Figure 17** Edward Hopper, *Early Sunday Morning*, 1930. © Whitney Museum of American Art, New York.

*Truck and Sign* is not *Early Sunday Morning*. The photograph is busy, it is loud, it is declarative, and at the same time it betokens a culture of resistance, of repression, that is as much a description of the traumatic as might be an environment of surrender, exposure, revelation. This precisely is the symptom of trauma: the simultaneous necessity of repression and the foregrounding of the very ways in which repression is impossible.[5] The charge to document a social trauma on the scale of the Depression, whether at the behest of others or as a description of the artist's intentions (conscious or not), could gain legitimacy only if a means was found by which that relationship could be recorded. Evans searched for such a solution from the outset of his practice. According to conventional wisdom, he might have argued that such an idiomatic expression of photographic potential was inherent in the work of a progenitor such as Eugène Atget. This is debatable. Atget would likely have been horrified, would have felt assaulted by the sign in *Truck and Sign,* the maiming of words and letters in *Luna Park,* the momentary freezing of time and its simultaneous inference of passage in *Lunchroom Window* (figure 18).[6]

Atget was after the almost sedentary traces of history (figure 19); Evans seeks the signs of an assault on those traces, seeks those moments in which history seems impossible, belied by the seemingly sedentary, established, absolute, final. There is something violent in the way Evans's photographs address the viewer. The photo seems surprised, injured even, by our presence, and in turn we are startled, if not assaulted, harassed, or even wounded by it. In turn, the photograph's inanimacy is its deferral of the traumatic so absolute to its own gradual emergence to the light of day, the light of experience.

If Evans's work can claim documentary status in the first year of the Depression, that status is secured only in an argument for what it is we might think that the photographer or even the photograph held to be documented. Our insecurity over this claim is as much a sign of the photograph's status as any assertion of what is represented. Were we to depend on the photograph for documentary value, we would have to confess that *Truck and Sign* isn't of much use at all: a sign, a couple of men, a partially visible truck, half or

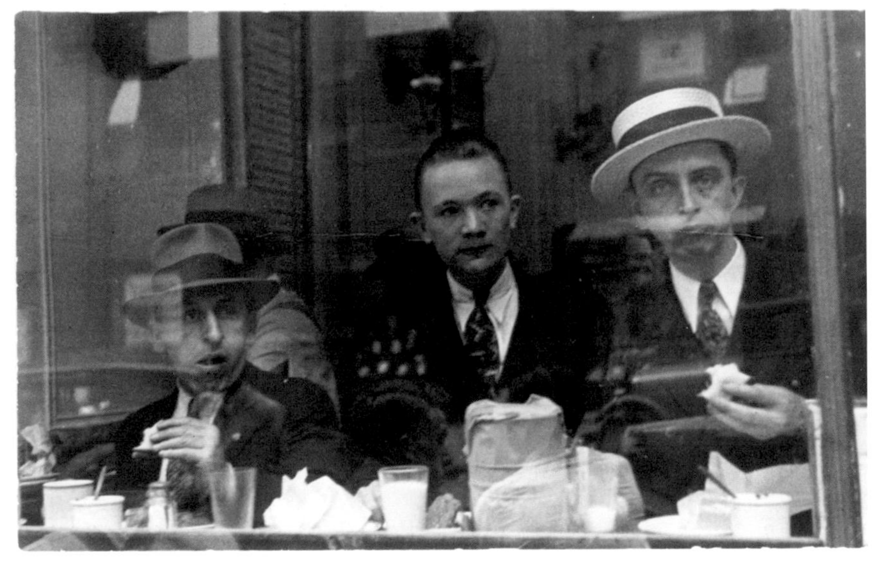

**Figure 18** Walker Evans, *Lunchroom Window, New York,* 1929. © Walker Evans Archive, The Metropolitan Museum of Art / Art Resource, NY.

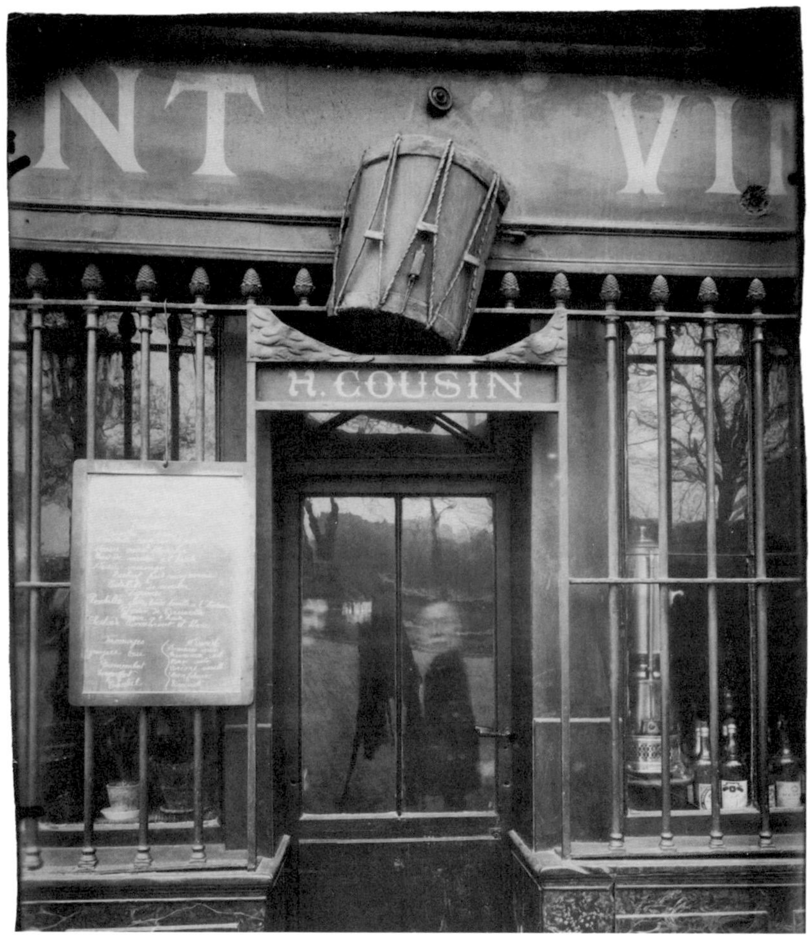


**Figure 19** Eugène Atget, *Au Tambor, 63 quai de la Tournelle (5e arr)*, 1908. Courtesy of George Eastman House, International Museum of Photography and Film.

one-third or one-tenth of a word or name spelled above a storefront. We can't be sure of the relations to the extent that they add up to a truth, a narrative or a record of something we understand, just as we can't be sure of adequate support for the sign itself, as if damage—form and content—emerges from precisely this condition, a radical uncertainty that always seems incongruent with the fact of the image.

The web of contradictions that is the truth of *Truck and Sign* may reveal trauma, the "damaged," as the material of documentary photography. But we must be careful not to assume that the understanding of trauma in Evans's work is the result of formula. If we attribute to Evans some sense of initial foray into these concerns in work as early as *Luna Park,* we must also differentiate his increasing commitment to the traumatic that unfolds alongside the Depression from moments wherein his predilection for the qualities of representation are perhaps emergent but somehow not yet as fully formed as in his mid-decade FSA work.

This cautionary tale is worth telling even in the face of *Truck and Sign.* For all its still-tentative forays into the terrain of the traumatized, the image is about a deeply self-conscious approach to its own making. For every previously noted uncanny detail, a moment or motive of supreme picture making is in play. The diagonal of the sign's carriage against its planar, friezelike expanse is straight out of formalist accounts of painting until the 1920s; it is almost as if Evans is cooking up a recipe out of Heinrich Wölfflin for the ultimate melding of Renaissance and Baroque form.[7] To assume that the documentation of the Depression would entail Evans's immersion in the traumatic would require both a greater resistance to formulas and a greater sense of why the formulas might not so readily work to embody a subject apparent only to its own symptoms of representation. Some kind of distinction is required between the commencement of a career and the establishment of a style, a practice.

Evans himself would come to privilege the term *documentary style.*[8] It implies a tool wielded and brought to bear, a bending of document to individuation and a bending of aesthetic to fact, or at least phenomenon. The phrase itself begs the status of intervention, or, more violently, the clashing of two sets of expectations normally content to hold their opposite corners in the wrestling ring of representation. An aspect of the traumatic seems immanent in the mode itself. This is apparent in *Truck and Sign,* in a particular quality of the intermingling of form and content.

The expanse of the sign is offered to the viewer as part of a continuum that is bordered by the back of the truck on the right and by both the workmen and the space behind them on the left. The question is raised as to whether the men are halted in their action, almost as if posing, or in the process of moving the sign on or off the truck. Is this a picture of delivery or removal? Is the passage of time a given, or invisible, or halted somehow? Do the imputed incompletion of the truck and the empty space to the left of the figures render these questions unanswerable? On each side of the seeming continuum, the bearings of sight, as well as materiality, are lost. A deeply destabilizing vacuum or void opens in the place of measure, story, drama, sense.

Much of the effect of the photograph depends on the relationship between knowledge of its status in the moment and lack of knowledge of just precisely which moment is depicted. Here the lie is given to photography's claim to the documentary: it must always err on the side of artifice. We always know that the photograph offers the viewer a moment in time, but we can never know the moment in question. This is not to ask for a reorientation of photography's hermeneutic, wherein the object is situated only in its moment of reception.[9] It is rather to say that when a moment is lost, its implication in the reality of a photograph is not enough to restore that time to the status of subject, or document. The continuum of a lived experience is ruptured somehow by and in the photograph, in much the same way that trauma damages the lived time of the victim, the victim's ability to imperceptibly place himself in what would normatively be experienced as his time (to have consciousness) to such an extent that his life becomes photographic instead of lived. Not memory in the normative sense, photography is traumatic. Its status as document is always denied at the same time as it seems well established.

The look of Evans's photographs, from the outset and increasingly into the 1930s, is that of the temporal bent out of shape. (Taken together, the three extant versions of *Truck and Sign,* showing successive moments in the loading of the "Damaged" sign onto the truck, are testimony to Evans's interest in the changing face of his subject, the extent to which each photographic moment fails to exist ever again. One can almost imagine the photographer creeping along the time-space continuum, determined not to miss a single temporal fold as experience reveals itself shutter click by shutter click.) Frontality speaks to a struggle to keep directly focused a subject that willfully seeks to slip the knot of servitude to the gaze. The workmen in *Truck and Sign* seem almost to be struggling to orient the "Damaged" sign correctly for the viewer, seem to be struggling to establish the photographic format itself.[10] They frame their actions; their actions are framed. And yet our inability to particularize their moment, to keep their time, opens the traumatic gulf between viewer and viewed that is as much the documentary quality of the photograph, its clinical status, as anything else.

ONE OF THE QUALITIES OF CONSCIOUSNESS with which trauma wreaks most havoc is time. All sorts of temporal expectations are denigrated when traumatic experience fastens its hold on being, in part as a result of the sheer failure to process so significant an occurrence and in part because of the symptoms of that failure.[11] It stands to reason, then, that historical time and its artifacts might also be tampered with, or at least reshaped in traumatic time, so as to become unrecognizable. Along the way, something like the history of art might lose its shape and form as well—might come to fail to offer up solutions to the visualization of disaster, might go in search, might wander toward an image willfully ignorant of tradition, when history seems just the culprit stealing time in the face of trauma.[12]

Measuring traumatic time is a difficult business; it is what psychoanalysis tries to do. It might seem, in the evisceration of the subject that characterizes much trauma etiology, in the elevation of the desire to keep the subject at bay—as its rearing up might promise the revisitation of the original event, beyond reach, something activated only if the stopped time of trauma itself is reactivated—that trauma as history might not be available to conventional modes of explication. What is resisted is narrative, that mode by which we assume history will reveal itself discursively. Failing over and over again to tell a story is one sign of trauma's hold; another is misrecognition of the component parts of a story waiting to be told.

After a time, Walker Evans stopped telling, or trying to tell, a particular story about image making. He resisted, in other words, the history, or a history, of art in favor of a practice that, while never claiming any kind of purity of documentation as its intention, nevertheless advertised some kind of avoidance of picture-making practices that might acknowledge the extent to which traditional narrative devices were highlighted as useless for conveying trauma in history. He stopped trying to make paintings out of photographs.[13] (Thus the importance of, the insistence on, words and letters for his images. Time and time again, rather than tell us something whole, words and their attendant forms tell us of their failure to add up, their failure to document.)

Despite my reading of *Truck and Sign,* photographs like *Lunchroom Window* and *Luna Park* bear scrutiny along these lines. The pictorial is paramount here. Whether trading in the found cubist language of fragmented signage or enhancing surface by slick feints of reflection and surprise—a palimpsest of visual layers suggesting the accumulation of pigment on canvas—these photographs bear a strong relation to a modernist tradition still founded on the prerogatives of painting. It's not simply that they take time to read, or at times seem to confound reading, but that they take a certain quality or type of time to read, a time that over its course conjures the temporality of the image's making. They unfold by layers, or fit together (even fail to fit together) piece by piece rather than render a single impression made up of myriad repetitions.

They suggest an image open to recessional penetration and in turn a ground built up temporally toward an apex that is image, composition, and framework as well as address to a viewer. Density of material is all in the superimposition of refraction on refraction or the overlapping of form on form. Multiplicity, repetition compulsion are moot; now tactics of analysis denied the gaze in ways that would diminish for Evans further into the 1930s.

The menus in the background of *Lunchroom Window* and the horizontal row of dentals in the architectural detail of *Luna Park* are cases in point. These are truncated repetitions; their accumulation is qualified, in the lunchroom window by the milky pool of reflection that blurs the readability of the plates on offer, in the pediment by the abrupt framing of left and right edges, and by association with other, more readily apparent fragmented forms, which speak more directly to the stoppage of counting than to its infinity. Instead of words (or objects, forms) repeated, as in a later photograph like *General Store Interior, Moundville, Alabama* (figure 20), we have words sliced off at each end. Instead of forms' attaining their totality in shapes that secure their status as goods, we have partial geometries—babble as a result of half articulation, as opposed to a type of visual Tourette's syndrome or stutter, as we have in *General Store* or *Factory Street in Amsterdam, New York* (figure 21), of 1930. Both of these images demand that we count until a type of exhaustion sets in, a kind of blockage, resistance, or repression beyond which cognition cannot continue, and only continues in the form of repetition—"OK, OK, OK, OK"; "1, 2, 3, 4, 5, 6"; this many windows and that many bricks.

To this extent, and *pace Truck and Sign,* Evans's earlier images tell us little about the traumatic—perhaps they have no need to—and instead embed the eye in the aesthetic, expelling some aspect of documentation at the same time. By 1929 or 1930 they risk the record of fact in favor of realism, as understood in the history of painting—as something as much about beauty as materialism. A predilection for the momentary compounds this impression. Neither *Luna Park* nor *Lunchroom Window* attempts to say anything about the eternal. We get the fragmented, cropped passing view of the amusement park's

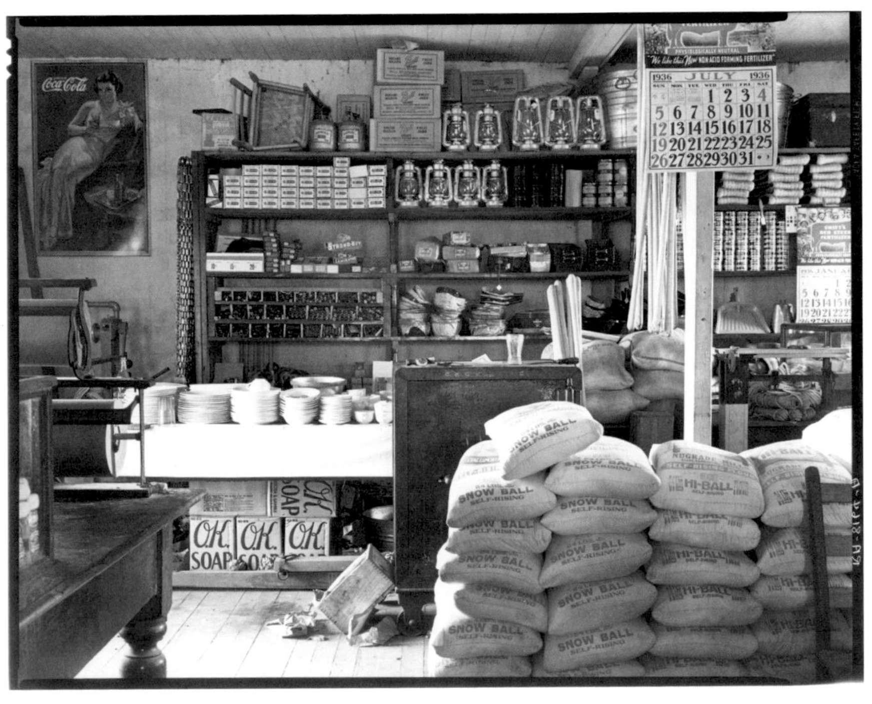


**Figure 20** Walker Evans, *General Store, Interior, Moundville, Alabama,* 1936. Library of Congress.

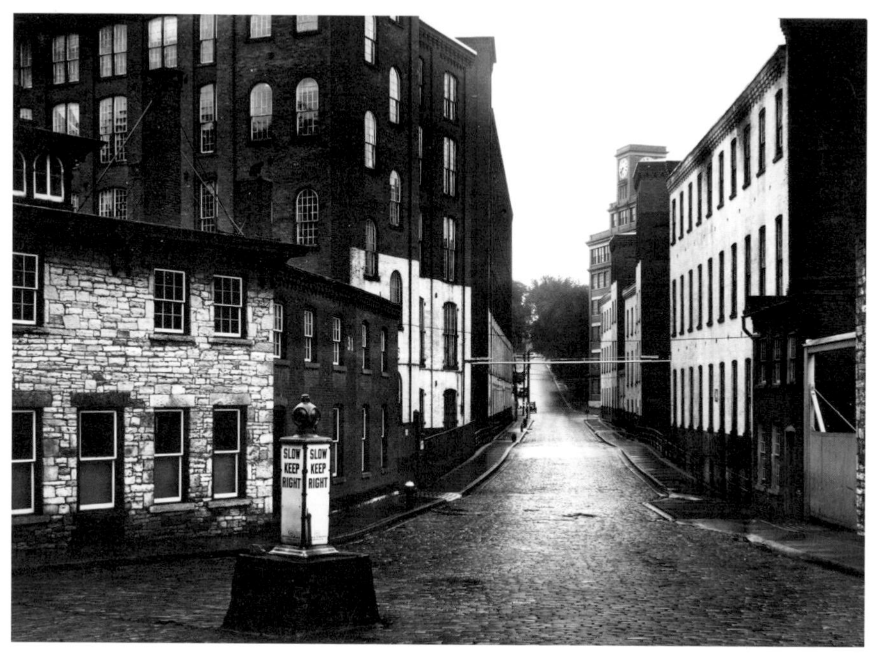


**Figure 21** Walker Evans, *Factory Street in Amsterdam, New York,* 1930. Gelatin silver print, 14.8 × 20 cm. Gift of Mrs. James Ward Thorne, 1962.171, The Art Institute of Chicago. Photography © The Art Institute of Chicago.

self-announcement, neither past nor future but only instantaneous present. Or we see the denizen of the diner in mid-chew, mid-gape, mid-glance. Infinity, the enslavement of time, is not necessary here, is not possible, is not felt. There is something of the ephemeral to these images that has nothing to do with trauma. The air that circulates through and around them is light, translucent, transparent even. The eternal does not reference transcendence, in other words: quite the opposite where trauma is concerned.

This is hardly the case in *General Store,* where an entropic heaviness of atmosphere echoes, and is echoed by, the leaden weight of the safe itself, cowering in the middle of the scene, or the dead weight of the flour bags, the stacked dishes, the boxes of soap. Alongside this sheer physicality of repetition there is the infinity of addition. The math is different here. Nothing in *Lunchroom Window* is repeated. Each figure wears a different hat, a different tie, is caught at a different stage of lunch, of eating. All the details across the foreground plane are distinct. You can count these, too, but they don't repeat: coffee cup, salt shaker, empty milk glass, sandwich wrapper, full milk glass, lunch pail, partly full milk glass, plate—all as differentiated as the three individuals shown. The possibility of individualism seems still redolent here and in *Luna Park,* where each fragment highlights another unique moment, not only in time but in space and matter too, whether or not we can identify what whole word, object, or function it fragments from. And the individuation of what we take to be the diner's main subjects is reinforced by the reflected heads in the bottom register of the photograph, shaped differently, bespeaking individual geometries of cranial formation, individual personalities, even in the most momentary of depictions. We almost feel we could identify these figures in a police lineup; we almost feel we are looking in a mirror.

*General Store* and, presciently, *Factory Street* are about a sameness, a paralysis that cannot be escaped, that cannot be adequately analyzed to the point of solution.[14] They are without solution and yet begging for a solution, while *Lunchroom Window* and *Luna Park* can live without one. Repetition compulsion, the inescapability of something never fully processed, the constant deferral of experience—all are classic traumatic symptoms, and all are central to the drive, or lack thereof, of these two pictures, imparting a certain neurotic quality to the frontality, the facing quality of the image, which is significantly less present in *Luna Park* and *Lunchroom Window*. Each image of this sort seems to radiate a sense of not knowing itself, as if its being is somehow behind its appearance but not apparent to it, as if what's depicted is merely a cover for something that isn't, a layer in front of another, a reality split from one that cannot be seen or measured. In this way, a thematic of loss is central to the apprehension of those Evans images most touched by the traumatic. Some truth central to these photographs is decidedly absent, in the same way that it is nearly impossible to give voice to trauma in its moment of occurrence.

We might benefit, then, from reading a more recent critic looking at Evans's FSA work for the exposure of trauma, however antithetical that exposure might be to the author's own interpretive intention: "The further one penetrates, the more one is rewarded by the minutiae of detail suspended in the seemingly transparent emulsion. We seem to experience a loss of our own reality; a flow of light from the picture to us and from ourselves into the picture."[15] At first the statement seems deeply rational, poetic even, structured as if to reveal some great truth about the image and the viewer's relationship to it, some kind of ultimate collectivity of encounter and response, redolent of a social dynamic enfolding class struggle, dream, wish fulfillment, and a collective unconscious. Yet as one penetrates further, something profoundly disorienting emerges from the discourse of the critic. He is at once in the picture and outside it, full up and at a loss; bathed in the radiance of light emanating from the image, and rendered invisible; capable of illumination himself, and absent.

Something dysphoric is at hand here: a concatenation of cognitive and emotional states and phenomenological conditions that seems closer to calibrating a kind of vertigo than a firmly grounded aesthetic. The ground on which the critic stands is destabilized: the photograph has done something almost violent to the writer's ability to wring coherence from appearance.[16] Despite the claim to see what Evans's work is about, there is an emptiness to the assertion, so that the only phrase that rings true, or climbs out of the state of paradox in which the writing is bathed, is "a loss of our own reality." This is a classic articulation of traumatic dislocation, of a type of numbing and dissociation common in the culture of trauma, gaining articulation here as a result of encounter with Evans's images.

The critic is looking at photographs more akin to *General Store* or *Factory Street* than to *Lunchroom Window* or *Luna Park*.[17] In their offering of a different version of complexity, these latter photographs reveal enough contradictory motives, effects, and juxtapositions to argue for a simultaneity of density, thickness of reference, and lack of problematic. Their mystery, in other words, is aesthetic—carried by a quality of surface or indistinctness of detail, as in the haze of reflections and veiling in *Lunchroom Window* or the incompleteness of form assuming completion in geometry in *Luna Park*—rather than pathological, or clinical, a word Evans had access to as early as 1931 to describe something of what he was after in his emerging practice, and which seems more appropriate to *General Store*.[18]

The proximity of narrative is much greater in *Lunchroom Window* and *Luna Park*. These photographs more readily suggest story, whether in the links made by the latter image to a cubist drama that unfolds over time in art history or in the reference to the passage of time that is so unavoidable in the former. Narration—life—goes on. In *Factory Street* and *General Store,* narration is stymied by the multiplicity of elements resisting resolution. Discerning beginning, middle, and end is impossible because there is no leverage with which to incite the passage of time and no hinge on which to hang its culmination in an experienced or putative conclusion. That is why counting is so important, as is the case in traumatic experience. The loss of temporal reference occasions a repetitious counting that can have no end because the scale of trauma is by nature overwhelming. Thus it matters little that the calendar in *General Store* gets the viewer from one to thirty-one, gets the viewer from the end of June to the edge of August: the implication of a monthly calendar, despite the distinction of proper names for different months and days and numbers, is that it will all just start again rather than simply end or come to conclusion, resolution, or the now so fashionable word *closure.* The calendar is anarrativistic, in other words. It manages time in the face of the ultimate temporal trauma: the end of time, or the inability of time to move because it has already ended, in perhaps a traumatic moment still only poorly held or understood, barely even revealed but somehow felt, somehow formed by affect, a quality that Evans's photographs have in excess while seeming always affectless.

Thus, it is possible, in the midst of a kind of orderly chaos wrought from the abstractions of accumulation and mathematical volume, to accord great volition to the narrative formation hidden in *General Store.* The tragedy of the safe amid the repetition compulsions of the rest of the image represents a kind of allegory of the Depression, wherein the formerly secure housing for assets now supports only detritus and is mostly hidden behind the infinity of goods drained of meaning by customers' diminished purchasing power. Yet even this feeble attempt to wrest story from the space of its evisceration comes across as deeply banal and on some level an admission of the impossibility of allegory. There is something farcical in this detail in the same way there is something farcical in the gorgeous texturing of the street and the building materials in *Factory Street* or *Washstand in the Dog Run and Kitchen of Floyd Burroughs' Cabin* of 1935–36 (figure 22). We are asked to question the status of the documentary when an element of its ridicule seems apparent.

What can possibly be the truth of such caressing of the eye, such cultivation of the palpable textures of surface and material in the midst of such emptiness and irresolution of reference? The comedy of narrative in each of these images is precisely a comedy of form; a way of saying by the very means of banality and melodrama of aesthetics how impotent is form in the face of the traumatic, of the Depression. The aesthetic is too obvious in the images that seem to add up intractably but undeniably to some kind of immeasurable truth of the historical moment.

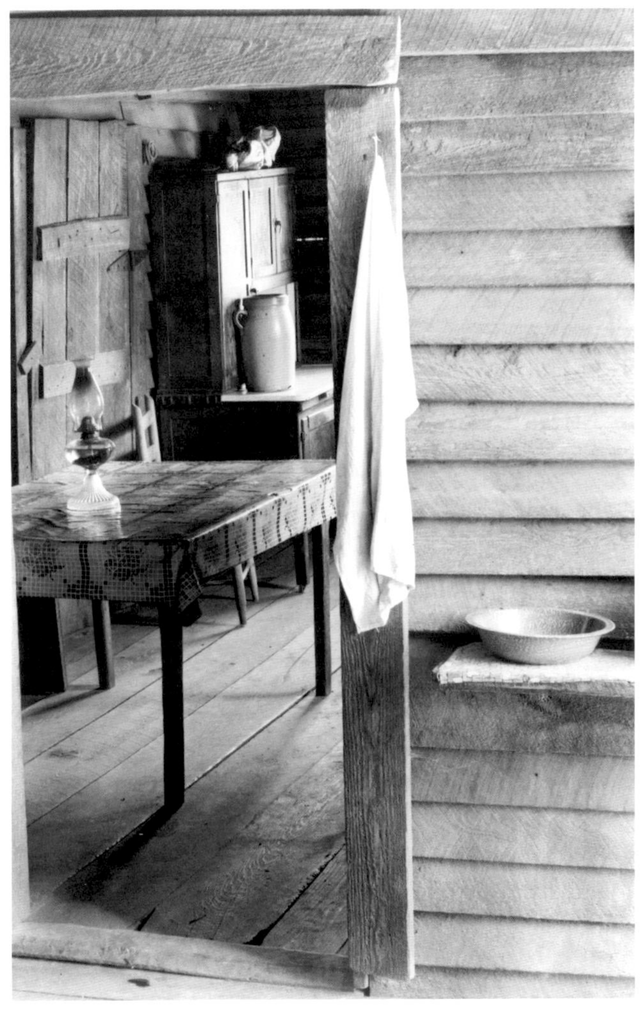

**Figure 22** Walker Evans, *Washstand in the Dog Run and Kitchen of Floyd Burroughs' Cabin, Hale County, Alabama*, ca. 1935–1936. Library of Congress.

In turn, there is nothing farcical, there is no need for farce, in *Lunchroom Window* or *Luna Park*. Their aesthetics seem normative, less strange, or perhaps strained, more seamlessly entwined with meaning and story, setting and composition, more at ease with a high modernist narrative enfolding everything from cubism to surrealism into its purview. As the aesthetic, the formal perhaps, seems part and parcel of meaning, so beauty or attraction make sense as and seem part of a larger canvas of representation.

In turn, in *General Store* the formal is crude, flattened, coarse even, the picture of Lincoln Kirstein's statement, in the essay he wrote for the Museum of Modern Art's *American Photographs* exhibition of 1938, concerning the time Evans captured with his photographs, of an "epoch so crass and so corrupt that the only purity of the ordinary individual is unconscious."[19]

In *Factory Street,* abstraction, aesthetics, and the formal seem almost obscene, an entanglement from which one cannot escape, threatening to strangle the viewer, a new kind of Laocoön. Certain of Evans's images seem, in other words, uncomfortable in their own skin, the skin of history of style. They are (especially *General Store*) like awkward family portraits, uncomfortable before the camera, mistrusting its intentions; all elements are lined up in their finery but reveal nothing, save for anxiety, exacerbation, and perhaps a type of madness. If we must wheel the history of art back on stage to make the point, they are something like Goya's royal family portraits.

Finally, anxiety as photographic trace seems most revealing of the traumatic in such work. In *Factory Street,* the facades are made to crunch together to fit the opening of the lens. Such subtle cantileverings of materials seem unlikely in reality, forcing an impression of photographic manipulation; the variety of facades seems staged, as if part of a set, a wall of surfaces behind which there is only a support scaffolding, as if on the lot of a movie studio. The stress of deciding how to enter the image is enough to turn the eye away—from the left or the right? Around the traffic sign, and if so, which way? A funnel effect promises to shoot vision into a narrow passage much less capacious and aerated than the foreground, whose resolution, whose diminution, is made by an incline that commences only once we leave the space of the built environment and enter that frame bordered and roofed by landscape, a funny articulation that seems to promise aerodynamic lift away from and out of the rest of the scene, like some sort of ramp to heaven—to the past, to relief, and yet to nowhere. This sounds melodramatic, but it is the cost of narrative's loss that such a pitch of meaning should be aspired to and suggested rather than more firmly secured. In those photographs where trauma appears to be a part of the formal fabric of the image, meaning is something felt only in aspiration.

In Evans's images of trauma, there is an inordinate amount of accumulation, of building up the stuff of the image, of stacking and piling and jigsawing into adjacency and bulk, mass, matter, as if this might substitute for meaning, for narrative, for the inaccessibility of language, for the loss of the human as animate agent, for the loss of the human as a sign of figuration. The most overwhelming stress imparted by these images is very much the result of a search for figuration away from the human, the body, as prototype. The project might be how to build a world when being is lost; how to photograph a world where being is denigrated so deeply that stuff is all that is left; how to measure affluence without anyone to spend or buy it; how to activate work with no workers, or workers without work. If trauma has a form in these images, it is written away from the body: it is a body that can't write itself, a body that has no place in the world it has yet made.

We are loath to enter these images for fear of violating a space that cannot recognize our physicality. These photographs are not made to be entered. In trauma, violation and exposure are significant effects.[20] Photographs like *Factory Street* and *General Store* are made up of a dance between exposure and violation. They bespeak forbidden spaces, yet these are environments that most certainly have been entered. They are built, they have stuff in them; the stuff and the buildings have been placed before us by human beings. And yet they are empty, empty of us, empty of humans. Hence these images are quite literally, and variously, "after the fact." Their belatedness is their quality of the past. The factory street seems abandoned; the utilitarian meaning of the general store

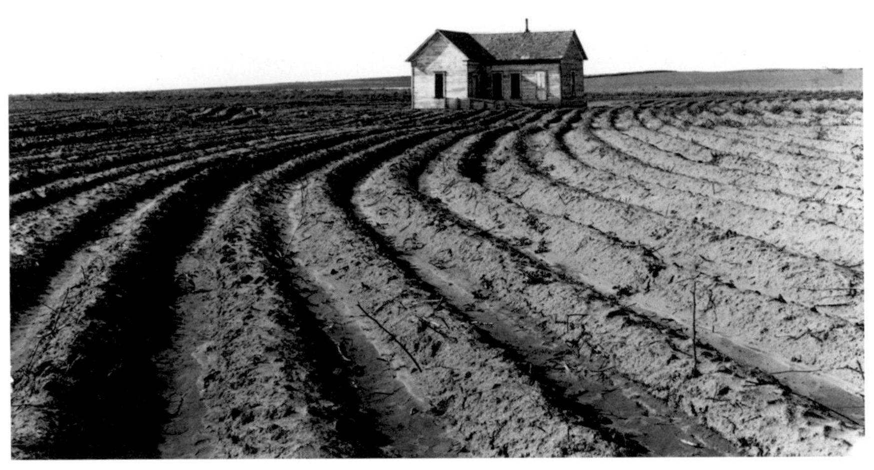

**Figure 23** Dorothea Lange, *Power Farming Displaces Tenants from the Land in the Western Dry Cotton Areas, Texas Panhandle*, 1938. Library of Congress.

is lost without consumers; the safe is impotent. The goods sit on the shelves; they have no agency, no volition, no metaphor of functionality. They are broken in their wholeness, in their repetition, in their facticity. The stuffs may have purpose, but they do nothing, and nothing is done with them. Fulfillment—historicity, the term Sara Blair privileges so well, so rightly, to characterize the work of Aaron Siskind and Ben Shahn—is impossible, denied, especially when that place in which use might be enacted, the land itself, looks in the same moment like Dorothea Lange's *Power Farming Displaces Tenants from the Land in the Western Dry Cotton Areas,* of 1936 (figure 23).

OF COURSE THE MOST POTENT EMBODIMENT of stress and anxiety in each of Evans's images is the demand made on the eye to count. We don't naturally entwine the aesthetic and the mathematical, though perhaps on some unconscious level they are more closely aligned. Certainly plenty of ink has been spilled on the aesthetics of mathematics. But counting without end, as is implied in these photos, is another matter altogether. Immanuel Kant writes of a mathematical sublime, but he is talking of a kind of sheer cognitive exhaustion, as Neil Hertz puts it, that comes at the end of a process which over time reveals an inexhaustibility of object.[21]

In trauma, the inexhaustibility of object is always a priori. And I don't think Evans is after the sublime in his thematics of accumulation and counting. In romantic ideology, the sublime is always arrived at from a starting point of rationality—from the starting point of the Enlightenment, from an essay into discovery of the divine, the otherworldly, the vertiginous, perhaps at the end of the quotidian road, a road different from that which takes us into and out of *Factory Street.* Evans's images seem rather to exist as proof of an irrational that is beyond the frame—the containment of the image—and yet carried by the sheer demands placed on the eye to count, to work out what this might add up to or what that might compute as, and failing to do so not because of an arrival at cognitive exhaustion or amazement or wonder but from an inability to stop the counting, to realize its conclusion, to escape a type of madness of the infinite, lest the trauma be reenacted once again. Cognitive exhaustion is no rescue here.

THERE WAS LITTLE, IF ANY, SUBLIME CROSSING of the roads of Hale County, in Moundville, or in Amsterdam, New York, in the 1930s. Evans's *Railroad Station, Edwards, Mississippi,* of 1936 (figure 24), is a case in point. The composition resembles that of *Factory Street.* In this case, however, an almost infinite number of entry points and facilitations of recessional penetration determine the very structure of the photograph (the issue is hardly the need to "Slow keep right"): three tracks, three dirt paths between the tracks, a station platform on the right border, an axis made by a line of cars on the left-hand side. Evans is fascinated by the continual plotting of ingress and egress, liminal separations and actual emplotments of place determined precisely by whichever path is chosen. Again, the eye counts interminably: railroad ties, platform supports, cars, tracks, fence posts, telephone poles.

Evans's photographic eye is all-seeing, or wants to posit a fiction of being so, a seeming inability/desire not to repress. Repression seems often to fail anyway to curb traumatic experience, traumatic materialism (with trauma, repression, a normal defense against that which offers resistance to normative processing and remembering, is rendered ineffective even if often unavoidable). Some kind of recognition of presence as uncomfortably unbounded seems mobilized in Evans's practice; an inability to edit, a refusal of editing perhaps, so that the image is all about exposure in its most exacerbated form, crossing the threshold of revelation into the terrain of violation.[22] No surer differentiation exists between Evans's photography and painting as such.

For Evans, as often as not, composition, vantage point, detail, material, and setting all test photography's capacity not to miss anything in its purview. Nowhere is this more evident than in the background detail in *Railroad Station* that serves as the image's ultimate, if elusive, focus. As the lines of tracks

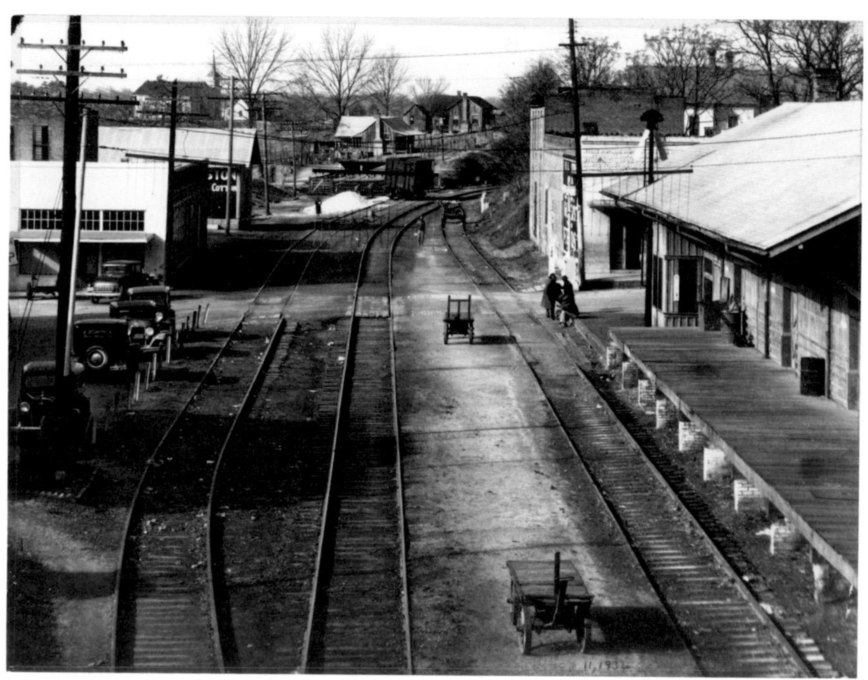

**Figure 24** Walker Evans, *Railroad Station, Edwards, Mississippi*, 1936. Photography Collection, Miriam and Ira D. Wallach Division of Art, Prints and Photographs, The New York Public Library, Astor, Lenox, and Tilden Foundations.

and paths begin to turn to the viewer's right, just before the putative horizon, a lone train car takes the center of the photograph. As if to ensure the omniscience of the shutter, however, at this instant something uncanny occurs. Rather than find this train car on the center track, the rail that leads the eye into the photograph from the foreground center, we locate the car on the track just to the left that has now turned into the background center of the picture. What is true at the outset of the image is no longer so. The photograph—all face—has performed its own defacement, has made apparent a wound to the reality previously assumed to be its documented material.

The model of trauma embodied in and by the photograph, the difficulties it proposes to adequately reading or seeing the image, is precisely a simulation, in a sense, of the radical rupture or disfigurement inevitable in the practice of looking and the demands it places on the concatenation of real and imputed temporal experiences that circulate through and around the experience of the photograph, given its claims to representation of some sort, to being *of* something. In short, the moment of looking is not that of the photograph, and yet it is only by stopping time that we can discern the elision that has taken place in the background of *Railroad Station, Edwards, Mississippi.* As time is mutilated in traumatic experience, in the actual physiological reconfiguration of the mind, so counting becomes a mode of both proving and being proved by the trauma (there is no end to it); perhaps gaining some foothold against it, drawing little circles of management around a psychic terrain that resists it, quite violently and for all intents and purposes intractably, ensuring that some control over the experience of time passing might be had, even if crudely. *Railroad Station* asks the viewer to count toward the moment of the uncanny, of the wound to the expected, the norm; and the eye counts almost interminably toward failure, toward violation of the expected.

Of course, temporally speaking, we meet the uncanny in *Railroad Station* in the future, at a point that we come to after entering the photograph in the foreground, at its face. The traumatic is held in abeyance, is deferred. One of the classic symptoms of trauma is its belatedness. We begin to lose the reality of the image after we arrive at a certain point, not just spatially or incrementally but in terms of the time it takes to come to that point where the train car starts to turn to our right and head out of the picture. From where the viewer stands, this moment is at least fictionally beyond the photograph's first moment, even if in reality that first moment is also always potentially the whole of the photograph or any moment in or of it. The suggestion of future, of moving beyond the time of the image, beyond even our own time perhaps, is all that is offered as a means of surviving the photograph.

And yet arrival at what others might call this punctum does not promise the future as release or relief.[23] (One of the charges of Roy Stryker to photographers in FSA employ was to document the relief efforts of the government.) However the future is inscribed in a photograph like *Railroad Station,* it is not a future to be aspired to. In traumatic experience there is a reason for this.

One of the ways in which trauma degrades normal temporal experience, sentience, or even consciousness is through its storage in an individual or social configuration of the future. Trauma is by definition an experience that is too overwhelming to be processed normally, to be made into everyday memory or recollection, because the recall is unbearable; it is experienced only in unconscious repetitions that feel more like reliving than memory or recollection.[24] And yet trauma is what it is only because it happened. Thus if it cannot be placed in the past, and if its existence in the present is unbearable, it must be held in the (mental) space of the future. But stored in the future, the trauma is always still to happen: it is no more bearable but just deferred, to some small extent, to an eternity of unbearable anticipation. Counting proposes a beginning and an end, even if the end never comes.

Though much Depression experience seems to trade on the aspirations attached to future relief and economic recovery, the calamity's tenacity, its seeming interminability, especially by the mid-to-late 1930s, ensured the necessity for housing the moment's reality, its belated emergence, its seeming unbounded presence, in the future. Only there might it be bearable, in the site where trauma is found, if it can ever be said to coalesce as object.

In trauma, relief, too, is always in the future: as trauma is housed in the future, held there, so suffering is in part imputed to be experienced in another time. Aspiration in and of itself is trauma to the afflicted. As the photograph is always another time, so its very form is traumatic and mirrors somehow the structure of such experience.

A passage from the *WPA Guide to 1930s Alabama,* published in 1941, which reproduces *General Store,* among many other pertinent photographs and illustrations, betrays a version of the circular thinking associated with trauma and to which the Depression lent its name as subject: "The future of farming in Alabama is unsettled. The manufacturing and mining industries are growing rapidly, while agriculture, shaken from its one-crop dream of cotton, gropes uncertainly. It is still the most important industry and will probably maintain this position for many years to come. However, its future will undoubtedly be more closely linked with the manufacturing industries—particularly since the establishment of the Tennessee Valley Authority with its program of abundant, cheap electrical power for both rural and urban sections."[25] Some kind of melancholy, some sense of failure, of the already assumed inability of the future to honor its promise of relief seems inherent in the writer's prose. A way of life is not simply passing: it has passed, and the hope of its revival, a hope that still takes shape in the way in which the passage clings to the agrarian dream, is revealed to be hollow.

The future should be savior, but when it is documented with accuracy, when "photographed," offered up in the literary equivalent of straight photography, in words contradictory and hesitant, the aspirational moment is full of a sense of another time that is really made up of slippages between past and present, bereft of ideology and capable only of an account stripped of the repression that might make such discourse into regionalist optimism rather than Depression reality, "unsettled," "shaken," uncertain.

Moreover, a new type of abundance is replacing that of the impotent version on offer in *General Store*'s implements, or apparent in the infinite but somehow past modes of entry—empty tracks, wagons, and automobiles as easily junked as not (see Evans's *Auto Graveyard*), men on foot loitering before or around, shambling toward a deeply qualified and uncertain future—that open so widely and deeply the image of *Railroad Station.* Cheap, abundant electrical power is the way of the future. Even the photograph and the camera seem obsolete, unable to ensure a future worth living for.

*Railroad Station, Edwards, Mississippi* is chock full of signs of belatedness, of history as the future, and an unbearable future at that. The image tells us as much of its past as of its moment. The photograph establishes the site as a stop on the railroad, but we pass through and by the depot as quickly as we identify it. The range of modes of transportation through the photograph is almost dizzying: five cars, two wagons, a boxcar of some sort, the foot traffic depicted by the cluster of (African American?) men in the center right of the image and the man walking in the background between the right and center tracks, the three tracks themselves, even the telephone lines carrying information into and out of the scene. All conspire to render Edwards as a site to be exited as rapidly as it is entered. Even the elevated viewpoint suggests that we are hovering above the scene, not of it: momentarily stopped, birdlike, before flying off in another direction.

The image's visual interest is obvious. A plethora of lines, contoured spaces, formal juxtapositions, and variegated materials create a scene as abstract as it is representational or figurative; it shows a hint of mid- to late 1940s Siskind *avant la lettre,* though such a reference only goes to secure the distance between Evans's work and what might be aptly called abstract photographism—the extent to which, for Evans, the impetus to narrative, to illustration, even perhaps to documentation, to detail, still holds as much ground as formalism itself.

In fact, some knowledge of the site may very well have informed the composition. The town of Edwards had been traumatically transformed well before the Depression. Edwards, originally called Amsterdam, failed to prosper adequately in the 1830s because the Alabama and Vicksburg Railroad bypassed it by roughly two miles. This remoteness, along with a cholera epidemic, led to the death of the original settlement. During the Civil War, a local railroad depot was burned by Union soldiers to prevent its aiding the Confederate cause.

The town and its area had been host to a plantation culture, but its African American population grew considerably as the Southern Christian Institute (later Bonner-Campbell College), a historically African American school, was opened in Edwards in 1882. The symbolic value of the railroad station, the railroad itself, and the fortunes of local African Americans, as well as slaveholders, Confederate soldiers, and the Union cause had historic as well as contemporary, Depression-era entwinement here.[26]

Stopping at Edwards, then, was complicated. Better to let the many ways into town carry one right out again, allowing vectors, like tracks, to cross, obscure the truth, render the future uncertain even as one chased it, on foot, by car, or by walking the rails, as so many did during the Depression. A few may even have ridden them as paying passengers, but a passenger train seems to be the one mode of egress not on offer here, despite its implication in station, tracks, and platform.

Evans himself likely came to Edwards by U.S. Highway 80, the Dixie Overland Highway, part of the first interstate system of roads inaugurated in 1926. U.S. 80 would, in fact, have run through both Edwards, Mississippi, and Hale County, Alabama. By 1927, the Bureau of Public Roads had this to say in a November press release titled "United States Routes Make Cross-Continent Run Easy": "Two . . . United States routes have a special interest for prospective transcontinental travelers living in the large eastern cities; one—Route 40—because it is the most direct motor route to California, and the other . . . 80—because it is a year-round road and, for the present at least, is more surfaced throughout than any other transcontinental highway."[27] By the apex of the Depression, transcontinental journeys would have trailed off a bit, but migrants would still have found this route of great appeal. In any case, it served Evans well: he seems to have used it as a type of Main Street by which to organize his wanderings and determine locations for his work in 1936. Traveling from Moundville to Edwards and back again was easier than other routes might have been at the time.

Evans's photo of Edwards documents something that is invisible to the naked eye, evades photography itself, while seeming immanent to it. The status of the documentary then assumes the structure of the traumatic—its invisibility, its deferral, its simultaneity of revelation and disguise. The photograph's claim to documentation is in the end a disfiguration of those very signs offered up literally by the image as the real, the remembered experience.

IN TURN, TRAUMA DENIGRATES the cognitive framework that holds history as something that might be documented or attain the status of document. History ceases to work. If history ceases to work, then might it not be possible that those forms instantiated by history as appropriate to a tradition of visual configuration should fall by the wayside, seem bankrupt, inadequate to the job—including the photo as document, and our very belief and investment in its truth?

In this context, those photographs by Evans that seem most directly to discard art history as a foundation for practice get closest to some kind of representational format and set of devices appropriate to a historical moment of significant rupture, upheaval, or violence. As already implied, *Factory Street* and *General Store* are two examples. Their basic frontality, their maintenance of the mathematical over the aesthetic or the mathematical as aesthetic, their inability to mobilize the signs (and their arrangement) that might ensure narrative, their banality of repetition and their denigration of the temporal, all speak to a system in resistance to the normal expectations of pictorial tradition.

Look by comparison at Dorothea Lange's most enduring image, her *Migrant Mother* (figure 25), arguably the most famous of all Depression-era photographs. Look at it especially alongside an image by Mary Cassatt (figure 26). The Cassatt could very well stand as a prototype for Lange, despite the dramatic class and historical differences between the two images. The formal mechanics and invention that identify the Cassatt as a modern reckoning with a particular theme or iconography are at play in the photograph as well. Lange, in fact, seems to mobilize a host of formal and psychological connections to

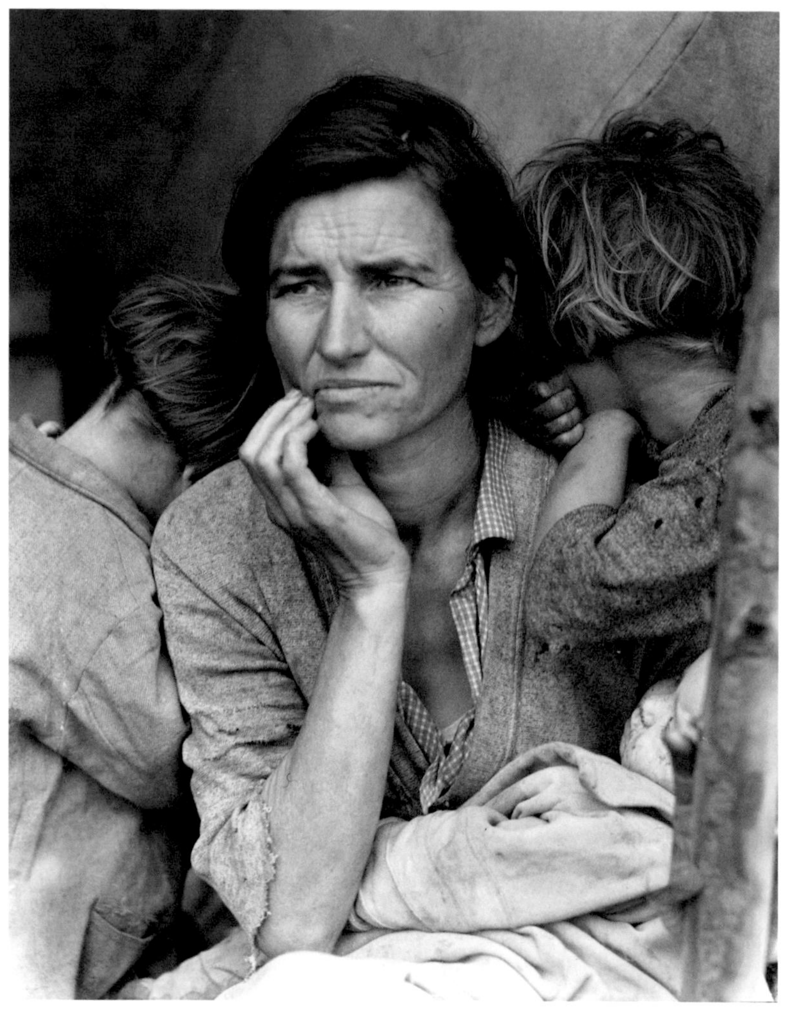

**Figure 25** Dorothea Lange, *Migrant Mother. Destitute Pea Pickers in California. Mother of Seven Children. Age Thirty-Two, Nipomo, California*, 1936. Library of Congress.

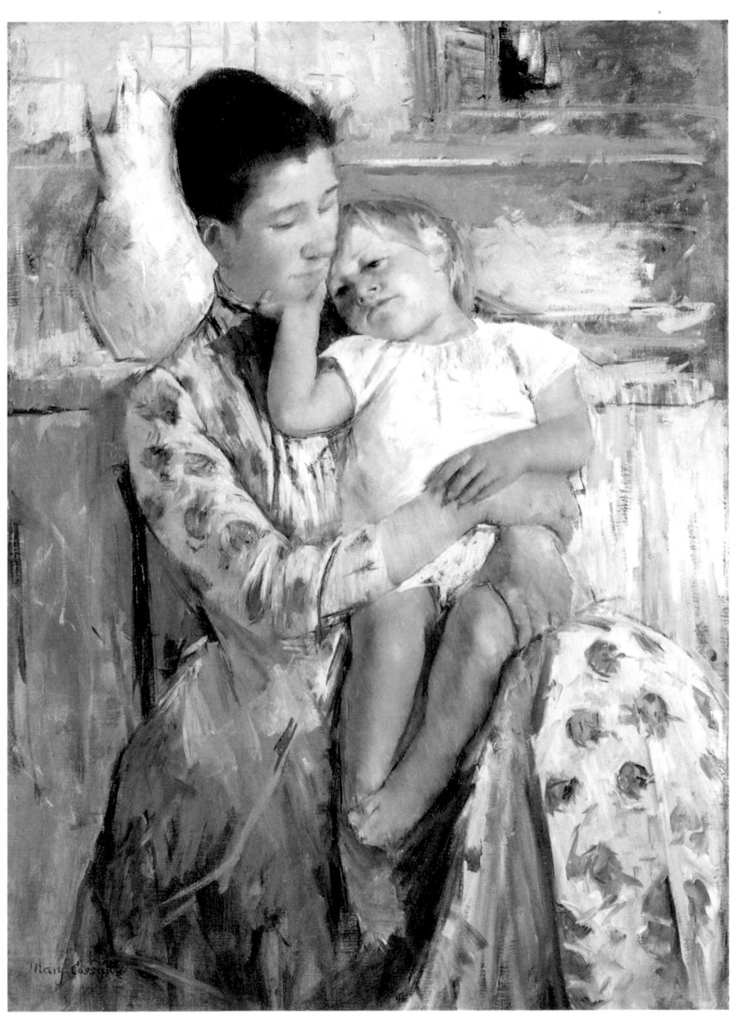

**Figure 26** Mary Cassatt, *Mother and Child,* ca. 1890. Roland P. Murdock Collection, Wichita Art Museum, Wichita, Kansas.

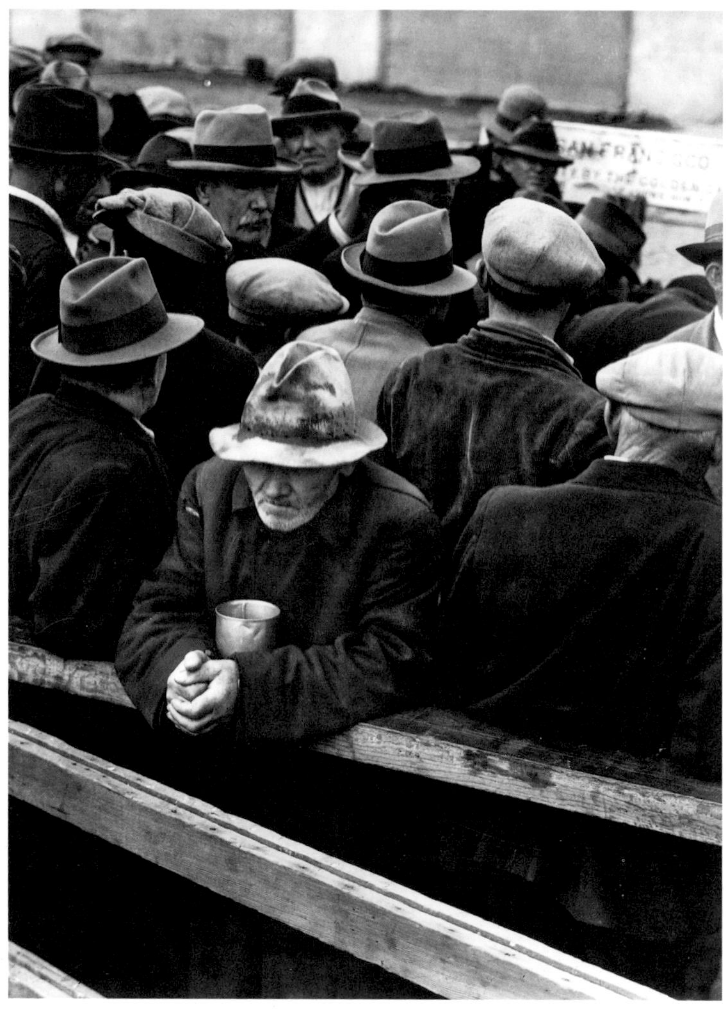

**Figure 27** Dorothea Lange, *White Angel Breadline,* 1933. The Dorothea Lange Collection, The Oakland Museum of California, The City of Oakland, Gift of Paul S. Taylor.

a tradition of picture making in order to ensure an elevation of subject beyond the circumstances of discovery in the material world. The history of art is very much present in Lange's image, and perhaps that is for the best. The ennoblement gained by such adjacency says something about survival, perseverance, spirit, and indomitability, all qualities that also have a place in an etiology of trauma: people do survive, and do so at times by the enactment of some or all of these qualities of being. In this sense, trauma perhaps accompanies rather than overwhelms existence. The point is that for Lange, certain notions of convention elevate something in the material of the Depression, remove experience and its image from the everyday, relieve the stress perhaps, turn the subject for a moment away from the trauma, as in her *White Angel Breadline* of 1933 (figure 27). Some breathing space is afforded, the counting is arrested, the repetition and the compulsions are ameliorated by the assertion of the individual and the notion of personal experience.

Consciously or unconsciously, in the intentions of the artist or the intentions of the object, Evans's work seems not to seek the same signs of history's hurt, as Fredric Jameson might put it.[28] Nor does this work seem to be in the business of alleviation, of therapy of any sort. Its abdication of history in its very complication of the historical is aligned with that of its subject precisely because no other solution seems viable, no other solution is felt. This is not heroic, it's just unavoidable, and it may even be the result of some aspects of Evans's personality that are less than appealing—something antisocial, misanthropic, that shaped his vision as fully as did the external world before his shutter.

Nor is it to argue for magical access on Evans's part to some kind of objective space of production outside history. In earlier work, the artist demonstrated every propensity for working within an aesthetic tradition, to offering fealty to certain expectations in order to practice within a history. But at a time when that history's dysfunctionality truly did overwhelm a system of subsistence, it must also on some level have seemed that the formal demands of that history were impotent, that they failed to get at something essential once in a while. In the recognition of such an opening into which some other version of trauma's appearance might creep, Evans seeded the ground for the occasional, skewed take on an extraordinary moment.

GENERAL STORE OFFERS STILL FURTHER EVIDENCE of this skewing. The photograph betrays a side that seems to have little to do with the Depression as trauma. Abundance is as evident here as deprivation or oppression, failure, or loss. The very specifics of a situation are embedded in the picture. Listen to a description from *The WPA Guide to 1930s Alabama:* "Left from Tuscaloosa on paved State 13 to MOUNDVILLE, 16.6 m., a progressive trading village serving a wider agricultural area. It has modern stores and homes, and is a shipping point for farm produce."[29] The guidebook gives an account of the general state of affairs of which Evans's image is a microcosm. Moundville is made to sound as if it melds past and present into a future modern and traditional, "progressive" and "agricultural." Mechanized, even machine-age means (shipping) of merging industry and the agrarian ideal come together with ancient forms of barter: it is a "trading village." The problem of the Depression is solved here, not exacerbated, and Evans seems for a moment to understand this, to seek the image of the site's reputation.

It would have been hard for him to miss it: the area was well known by the early 1930s as both a tourist destination and an archaeological site.[30] In fact, the guidebook goes on to account for this other aspect of Moundville's identity: "Right from Moundville on a graded dirt road to MOUND STATE MONUMENT, 17.5 m., one of the finest mound groups in the south. . . . The Moundville site supported a large population of agricultural Indians, who planted corn, made excellent pottery and possessed considerable artistic skill. Although there were small villages for several miles above and below the site, Moundville was the culture center and largest city of the region. The absence of European relics indicates that it was occupied in prehistoric times."[31]

Whereas the modern village is reached by paved road, the ancient monument is accessed by "graded dirt road." People of "considerable artistic skill" once worked the surrounding land. The meeting of modern, progressive capabilities and traditional, ancient, or perhaps even more primitive tendencies is implied for the historical site as well as the present day. Moreover, the site's historical status is secured by the archaeological, by the possibility of tourism, the need to see something of interest in this place.

All of a sudden Evans's photo itself takes on the status of archaeological excavation and, by extension, some kind of psychoanalytic exploration. An allegory of the site's original inhabitation pushes to the surface with the overabundance and repetition of stock. As if in deference to the environs' origins, *General Store* no longer belies the stereotypes of a Depression context but rather seems the entombed residue of a time unearthed, excavated by photography. Documentation becomes excavation. The general store is the burial mound of 1936 or 1941; the photograph is a leap into the future, that space where trauma itself is entombed, zeroing in on what's left of a culture whose passage is commemorated in its death, the death made flesh by the photograph. The sense of abandonment that accompanies the accumulation and multiplication of goods, that is housed literally in the identity of the safe and its impotence, reveals the site as past, as the result of traumatic passage and as documentary object, shard-like, and held in the space of the future, that space in which archaeology as document is made possible.

*General Store* posits time as a deeply complicated entity, never monodirectional, both synchronic and diachronic, or perhaps neither. The calendar in fact denies documentation as much as it suggests its possibility. The time may be July 1936, but the calendar gives no indication as to which day. Documentation might be the result of excavation, of archaeology, but its status is deeply qualified by the limits placed on the specificity of moment represented. This is in part the leitmotif of Evans's image, the pitfall inherent in the dependency on information, however vastly accumulated—a veiled critique perhaps of the job he had taken on for the FSA, of the adequacies of photography, however straight he too might have liked it to be. Traipsing around Alabama, he happened upon a site whose surface belies the depth of historical association that leads back to "prehistoric" moments, and yet he was forced to admit the failure of his chosen mode of representation to give up the character of the very moment in which he existed.

FOR EVANS, PHOTOGRAPHY AS DOCUMENT was an injury brought on by the bureaucratization of loss, not promise; history, not historicity. As a result, no American photographer of the 1930s begs more pressing, immediate, and in some ways vexing contrast with his peers, despite as well as because of the acute sense of "triangulation" that Sara Blair draws between Siskind, Shahn, and Evans. Blair can mobilize her argument so persuasively in part because Siskind and Shahn together reveal enough of a congruence, made out of momentary idiomatic expressions, with Evans's practice to have the three figures seem to represent a totality of documentary experience in the 1930s. There is something deeply useful and profitably complex about this formulation, as it asks us to consider what Evans has in common with these others as well as what differentiates him.

When we do draw certain comparisons between Shahn and Evans, the space between their work opens widely. Take Shahn's *Untitled (Lower East Side, New York)* of April 1936 (figure 14), and Evans's *Lunchroom Window* (figure 18). Both images are the result of what might be called street photography; neither ostensibly has the "permission" of its subjects. Each image is momentary, and Shahn's is even reminiscent of what he might have learned from Evans earlier in the decade, when the two were living together, and Evans offered up Shahn's only lesson in camera operation. Aside from a shared penchant for privileging language as much as human or inanimate material, the similarities end there. Shahn's connection to and with his human subjects, despite the cropping, fragmentation, and abstraction, is immediate and direct, implying the possibility of address, dialogue, interaction, and the dialogic. Evans's image resists all of this: it is constructed to render the uncanny the norm, so that the possibility of the social seems out the window, so to speak. Nothing in the Shahn necessarily implies any relation between the three frontal figures, and yet it takes a nanosecond to divine that their knowledge of each other, and us, is possible.

Nowhere does this seem the case in *Lunchroom Window,* and when we come to an Evans image of the same year as Shahn's, say *Sharecropper Bud Fields and His Family at Home, Hale County, Alabama* (figure 28), one of the most memorable and often-reproduced of the images from *Let Us Now Praise Famous Men,* the contrast with Shahn is that much more stark. Even in the family setting, in such physical proximity, genetic connection, and social suture, it is easy to surmise that these figures are strangers to each other, as well as to us—or perhaps more so. Experience—and by experience I mean their presence as part of this particular photograph—has driven them so far into themselves, predominantly formally, that connection seems impossible. Traumatic conditions of existence ensure a photography of deprivation—theirs and ours. In the end, a traumatic inanimacy prevails, a paralysis. The human is as intractably insular as the frieze of wall, doorway, and hanging objects that forms a backdrop to the Fields family. Impoverishment touches everything and everyone.

Shahn, on the other hand, as Blair so rightly makes plain, plots the space between Evans and Siskind, mining modernity's formal invention and iconographic materialism, its ironic proximity to the social and environmental experience of the Lower East Side, while retaining something of the narrative imperative necessary to the conviction that identity formation and facilitation are part and parcel of the photographic project, the documentary ideal.

EVANS WAS RECALCITRANT, EVASIVE, AND IRRESPONSIBLE with respect to others' expectations of him, and seemingly dedicated to an impassive, abstract, dispassionate image of the Depression and its trauma. Such a mien would seem to be at dramatic odds with those of Aaron Siskind, Ben Shahn, and even Dorothea Lange. In this view, the vivid and gripping notion of historicity with which Sara Blair invests the work of Siskind and Shahn, in Harlem and on the Lower East Side, would be anathema to Evans, might even get in the way of his intentions. Blair's argument, rigorous and moving, is all about the confluence of photography's plotting of coordinates and its subjects' investment in the same, in mapping the shutter's history and the immigrant's historicity,

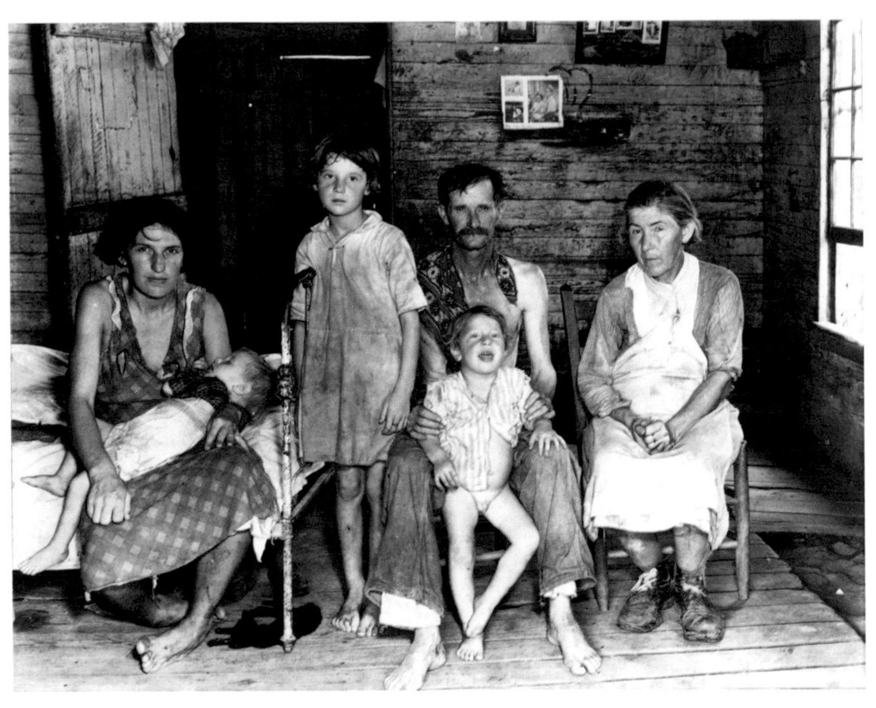

**Figure 28** Walker Evans, *Sharecropper Bud Fields and His Family at Home, Hale County, Alabama,* 1935–36. Library of Congress.

in modernity. Evans's work, on the other hand, seems more to essay the space between coordinates and their loss, their recession, their depression, perhaps into the past or simply as unavailable to identity formation in the present: their identity is already eviscerated, and photography is ill-equipped to determine how to give it back.

But lest we place the weight of Depression's trauma on the photographer alone, it is equally important to recognize the extent to which his work may have been tapping into a sense of the sheer materialism, the sheer economic desperation of the South, in the mid-1930s, compared to that of the Lower East Side or Harlem.

Listen to the Mississippi writer Eudora Welty, in her touching first short story, "Death of a Traveling Salesman."[32] The story first appeared on its own in 1936, the annus mirabilis of Evans's work in Alabama and Mississippi. Welty herself was a photographer and worked for the Works Progress Administration at times during the Depression as a publicity agent traveling around Mississippi (with a camera). The main character is a salesman, seeking direction from the people whose roads he travels in Mississippi in 1936. "He had made the Beulah trip before. But he had never seen this hill or this petering-out path before—or that cloud, he thought shyly, looking up and then down quickly—any more than he had seen this day before. Why did he not admit he was simply lost and had been for miles? . . . He was not in the habit of asking the way of strangers, and these people never knew where the very roads they lived on went to."[33] Welty describes an environment in which historicity is not an encounter with the world or the subsequent forging of a rapprochement between social condition, social origin, and neighborhood. Rather, the author accounts for the formation of self as utterly reduced to the most local and undistinguished signs, traces of coordinates, so that the subject never even knows the destination or origin of the road on which he lives; little is known beyond the beating of his own heart.

Welty writes a world defined precisely in the shadow of unmooring from any other imaginable place, reality, or connection. She writes of a place and a people with little or no imagination, let alone home, a people and place unmapped: "This desolate hill country! And he seemed to be going the wrong way—it was as if he were going back, far back. There was not a house in sight."[34] There could hardly be a more direct articulation of photography's failure to document in the face of trauma, of loss, or perhaps the failure of subject matter to offer itself up adequately to documentation. Its signs of identity are so meager as to fail repeatedly to point the way beyond the exact place in which one "lived."

Sara Blair rightly avoids associating the photography of urban assimilation, or even of the failure to assimilate—even resistance to the attempt—with something like Welty's intention. Welty's subject in this story, like Evans's subjects, leads from loss; Siskind's and Shahn's lead from gain, the sense that loss might or will be escaped and replaced rather than continually affirmed. This is not at all to judge one social situation or another: it is simply to confirm the very different quality of documentary offered up by these photographers and their subjects.

Evans, goes so far as to render his subjects unaware of the loss that defines them. Trauma's invisibility is intact rather than denied or actively struggled against, attacked even with and by what Blair calls Siskind's subjects' embrace of modernity, their belonging in it. Let us return to Evans's *General Store, Interior, Moundville, Alabama*. The obvious identification of loss and of impotence, the safe—now but a prop for haphazardly gathered detritus—is the most banal allegory in the photo, and yet it is utterly at odds with the rest of the image's almost pathological abundance. Something here has been ripped from life and clinically illuminated.

Siskind's two figures in *Sunday Afternoon: Mr. and Mrs. Joseph Metz* (from *Portrait from a Tenement*) (figure 3) of 1936, the same year as *General Store,* in Blair's beautiful words, "produce . . . the lived space they occupy," right down to the mobilization of psychic energy denoted by their absorptive comportment: they suggest that mind itself, individual and collective, healthy even, normative, is a part of the equation. This couple's documentary status is continuous with a story that narrates a time before and after the image (as well as the time of the image). Evans's photographs, peopled or not, offer neither. They are hopeless, as hopeless as the situation of Welty's salesman, seeking direction from the people whose roads he travels in Mississippi in 1936. To make this claim is not to attribute something anecdotal to the work of Siskind or the imputed lives of his subjects. Here, in Siskind, as in Shahn's work, narrative is an element indistinguishable from documentary; it *is* documentary. For Evans, the resistance of narrative, the failure to find story in his world, argues for the denigration of documentary intention in the face of trauma.

In closing, let us compare Evans's *Washstand in the Dog Run and Kitchen of Floyd Burroughs' Cabin* of 1935–36 (figure 22) with Siskind's *Untitled* (from *Dead End: The Bowery*) (figure 8). Siskind tells the story of the subject's struggle to both live with and achieve a place in history: time is a continuum with beginning, middle, and end. Trauma here is already being organized and diagnosed; the healing has begun, however large the job might seem. In Evans's work, each element resembles the subjects described by Welty's traveling salesman (a figure for Evans perhaps): "These people never knew where the very roads they lived on went to." We see bowl, wall, shelf, towel, table, pitcher, and other objects, but they stand unto themselves: they are parts of an image, to the extent that we consider the image willy-nilly a totality or unity, but they are detached and isolated in their abstraction and particularity. The acute grain of their textures is an argument for their distinction rather than their connection, their loss as much as their gain.

Let Welty, the writer, have the next-to-last word, from the passage just following her description of the ignorance of destination identifying the denizens of the world Evans was photographing at this very moment: "People standing in the fields now and then, or on top of the haystacks, had been too far away, looking like leaning sticks or weeds, turning a little at the solitary rattle of his car across their countryside, watching the pale sobered winter dust where it chunked out behind like big squashes down the road. The stares of these distant people had followed him solidly like a wall, impenetrable, behind which they turned back after he had passed." Like a wall, impenetrable, traumatized, photographed, undocumentable; "but then he had not even been close enough to anyone to call out."[35]

EVANS'S JOB TITLE, ASSIGNED TO HIM BY STRYKER in 1936, was "information specialist." An extraordinary title. Are we not all information specialists? What do we do, day in and day out, as the very fundamental definition of the normative, but process information, specialize in it? In trauma, however, we are robbed precisely of this specialization. Trauma is a condition that denies specialization and deprives one of information, of experience: it denies documentation. That is in part its terror. Even outside trauma, there seems a type of madness in the very articulation of the phrase *information specialist,* something almost Kafkaesque, suggesting one of an infinite number of clerks buried in a bureaucracy, rendered insane by their surroundings and occupation. But the bureaucracy itself was broken, and at times so was its image.

# Notes

*Sara Blair is grateful to Jonathan Freedman, Barbara Galasso, Howard Greenberg, Michelle Lamunière, Nancy Lieberman, Naomi Rosenblum, Kerren Sachs, and Anne Coleman Torrey for all their help in the coming into being of this work. Eric Rosenberg would like to thank Miriam Stewart for her support and encouragement. Kirk Eck, Barbara Galasso, Sonia Hofkosh, Nathan Kerr, Andrew Moisey, Naomi Patterson, Claudia Ponton, Laura Rubenstein, Blake Stimson, Eileen Sullivan, and Greg Williams also deserve Eric Rosenberg's gratitude.*

**Introduction**

1. For examples of scholarship on the FSA that covers these topics, see Sidney Baldwin, *Poverty and Politics: The Rise and Decline of the Farm Security Administration* (Chapel Hill: University of North Carolina Press, 1968), and Michael Grey, *New Deal Medicine: The Rural Health Programs of the Farm Security Administration* (Baltimore: Johns Hopkins University Press, 1999).

2. On the larger urge for "documentary expression," see the classic work in the field: William Stott, *Documentary Expression and Thirties America* (New York: Oxford University Press, 1973).

3. Ibid., 18.

4. Among the earliest and defined uses of the phrase, see John Grierson, "The Documentary Idea: 1942," in *Grierson on Documentary,* ed. Hardy Forsyth (London: Faber, 1979), 112–13.

5. James Agee, *Let Us Now Praise Famous Men* (Boston: Houghton Mifflin, 1941), 9.

6. The scholarship on FSA photography is immense and growing. Important works include F. Jack Hurley, *Portrait of a Decade: Roy Stryker and the Development of Docu-*

*mentary Photography in the Thirties* (Baton Rouge: Louisiana State University Press, 1972); Pete Daniel et al., *Official Images: New Deal Photography* (Washington, DC: Smithsonian Institution Press, 1987); Carl Fleischhauer and Beverly W. Brannan, eds., *Documenting America, 1935–1943* (Berkeley: University of California Press, 1988); James Curtis, *Mind's Eye, Mind's Truth* (Philadelphia: Temple University Press, 1989); Nicholas Natanson, *The Black Image in the New Deal: The Politics of FSA Photography* (Knoxville: University of Tennessee Press, 1992); Michael Lesy, *Long Time Coming: A Photographic Portrait of America, 1935–1943* (New York: W. W. Norton, 2002); Cara Finnegan, *Picturing Poverty: Print Culture and FSA Photographs* (Washington, DC: Smithsonian Institution Press, 2003); Beverly Brannan and Gilles Mora, *FSA: The American Vision* (New York: Harry Abrams, 2006); Stu Cohen et al., *The Likes of Us: Photography and the Farm Security Administration* (New York: David Godine, 2008); and Julia Foulkes, *To the City: Urban Photographs of the New Deal* (Philadelphia: Temple University Press, 2010). For other works that consider FSA photography in relation to other photographic practices, see Maren Stange, *Symbols of Ideal Life: Social Documentary Photography in America, 1890–1950* (New York: Cambridge University Press, 1989); James Guimond, *American Photography and the American Dream* (Chapel Hill: University of North Carolina Press, 1991); Lili Corbus Bezner, *Photography and Politics in America: From the New Deal to the Cold War* (Baltimore: Johns Hopkins University Press, 1999); and John Raeburn, *A Staggering Revolution: A Cultural History of Thirties Photography* (Champaign: University of Illinois Press, 2006). There is an even larger body of monographs concerned with the individual photographers who worked for the FSA. On these, an older though still useful bibliographic guide is Penelope Dixon, *Photographers of the Farm Security Administration: An Annotated Bibliography, 1930–1980* (New York: Garland, 1983). For the photographers considered in this book, see especially Walker Evans, *Photographs for the Farm Security Administration, 1935–1938* (New York: De Capo, 1973); and Deborah Martin Kao et al., *Ben Shahn's New York: The Photography of Modern Times* (New Haven: Yale University Press, 2000).

7. Howard Levin and Katherine Northrup, eds., *Dorothea Lange: Farm Security Administration Photographs, 1935–1939*, vol. 1 (Glencoe, IL: Text Fiche Press, 1981), 197–98.

### Against Trauma / Sara Blair

1. Roy Stryker, *In This Proud Land: America 1935–1943, As Seen in the FSA Photographs* (Greenwich, CT: New York Graphic Society, 1937), 7. Stryker goes on to note

that this vision "undoubtedly accounted for the great number of photographs that got into the collection which had nothing to do with official business" and for the "unusual continuity" of the FSA Historical Division file. Compare the advice of Rexford Tugwell, head of the FSA: "Show the city people what it's like to live on the farm." Cited in James C. Anderson, ed., *Roy Stryker: The Humane Propagandist* (Louisville, KY: Photographic Archive, University of Louisville, 1977), 4.

2. Stryker, *In this Proud Land,* 15. Nicholas Natanson, in *The Black Image in the New Deal: The Politics of FSA Photography* (Knoxville: University of Tennessee Press, 1992), 71, notes that the FSA archive, with its emphasis on land management and rehabilitation programs, lacks the "urban accent" of the Federal Writers' Project and other New Deal documentation. Both Natanson and Maren Stange, in *Bronzeville: Black Chicago in Pictures, 1941–1943* (New York: New Press, 2003) regard the Chicago-centered work of the Historical Division photographer Russell Lee as a corrective lens through which to read the FSA archive.

3. The discussion of the estrangement or resistance of Historical Section photographers to the logic of FSA production is ongoing and pointed. For example, in their introduction to *Documenting America, 1935–1943* (Berkeley: University of California Press, 1988), the editors, Carl Fleischhauer and Beverly W. Brannan, argue for scholarship that attends to series production as the key mode of FSA practice so as to emphasize the agency of the working "photographer in the field" over and against institutional aims (viii); Alan Trachtenberg, "From Image to Story: Reading the File," in the same volume (43–55), makes the case for reading FSA work in the context of the project "file," which juxtaposes notes and accompanying texts submitted by photographers (and thus, again, their resistance to institutional directive) with shooting scripts and negatives. The photographers I read here embody a far more categorical kind of estrangement or distance, one whose effects on the development of documentary practice have been a matter of increasing interest in recent years.

On the place of those not-quite-white Jews in photographic practice and institutions of the era, see Max Kozloff, *New York: Capital of Photography* (New York: Yale University Press, 2002); A. D. Coleman, "No Pictures: Some Thoughts on Jews in Photography," *Photo Review* 23, no. 1 (2000): 2–5; MacDonald Moore and Deborah Dash Moore, "Observant Jews and the Arena of Photographic Looks," in *You Should See Yourself: Jewish Identity and Postmodern American Culture,* ed. Vincent Brook (New Brunswick, NJ: Rutgers University Press, 200), 176–204; Robert Fulford, "Dream Merchants: Jews, Photography, and Andre Kertesz," *Queens Quarterly* 112, no. 2 (2005): 221–33; Sara Blair, "Jewish America through the Lens," in *Jewish in America,* ed. Jonathan Freedman and Sara Blair (Ann Arbor: University of Michigan Press, 2004), 113–34.

4. Jaromir Stephany, "Interview with Aaron Siskind," in *Aaron Siskind: Toward a Personal Vision, 1935–1955,* ed. Deborah Martin Kao and Charles A. Meyer (Chestnut Hill, MA: Boston College Museum of Art, 1994), 27–44 (quote, 41).

5. A detailed history of the Lower East Side as an iconic site is provided by Christopher Mele, *Selling the Lower East Side: Culture, Real Estate, and Resistance in New York City* (Minneapolis: University of Minnesota Press, 2005), particularly chapter 2, "Different and Inferior: The Ghetto at the Turn of the Century," 31–77. On the infamy of the Bowery as home to saloons, dime museums, flophouses and missions, blind pigs, clip joints, brothels, pawnbrokers, and shooting galleries as well as thieves' markets and tattoo parlors—but "never . . . a single church"—see Luc Sante, *Low Life: Lures and Snares of Old New York* (New York: Farrar, Straus and Giroux, 2003 ), 14.

6. Richard Doud, "Oral History Interview with Roy Emerson Stryker, 1963–1965," June 13, 1964, Archives of American Art, Smithsonian Institution, Washington, DC, www.aaa.si.edu/collections/oralhistories/transcripts/stryke63.htm.

7. Peter Kvidera, "Rewriting the Ghetto: Cultural Production in the Labor Narratives of Rose Schneiderman and Theresa Malkiel," *American Quarterly* 57, no. 4 (2005): 1131–54 (quote, 1135); Lucy Lippard, "Double Take: The Diary of a Relationship with an Image," in *The Photography Reader,* ed. Liz Wells (London: Routledge, 2003), 343–53 (quote, 346).

8. Nancy L. Green, "Sweatshop Migrations: The Garment Industry between Home and Shop," in *The Landscape of Modernity, 1900–1940,* ed. David Ward and Oliver Zunz (Baltimore: Johns Hopkins University Press, 1997), 213–34, explores the Lower East Side's historic apparel trade and its distinctive form, the sweatshop, as a definitively modern economic model. Christine Stansell, in *American Moderns: Bohemian New York and the Creation of a New Century* (New York: Henry Holt, 2001), emphasizes the ways in which the storied site of bohemian self-creation, Greenwich Village, was "proximate and permeable to the Jewish Lower East Side" (6), which "surged with the energy of a population on the verge of enormous achievements" (21) and offered genteel "native" Americans opportunities for both adventures of the rougher sort and experience of the radically new (for them) possibilities of café culture, free speech, literary

journalism, avant-garde drama, and more. A similar argument about the development of energies coalescing on the Lower East Side as a force in shaping the rise of Hollywood and a national mass culture is made by Paul Buhle, *From the Lower East Side to Hollywood: Jews in American Popular Culture* (New York: Verso, 2004).

9. Ironically, the Historical Section's success in making the representation of trauma central to its mission of documentation led Stryker himself to plead with his photographers for images of individuals who appeared not lost in time but plausibly assimilable to the New Deal project of modernization: "*We must have at once:* pictures of men, women and children who appear as if they really believed in the U.S. Get people with a little spirit. Too many in our file now paint the U.S. as an old person's home and that just about everybody is too old to work and too malnourished to care much what happens" (emphasis in the original). See Susan Sontag, *On Photography* (New York: Picador, 2001), 62.

10. Gordon Parks, from Martin H. Bush, "A Conversation with Gordon Parks," in Martin H. Bush, *The Photographs of Gordon Parks* (Wichita, KS: Wichita State University, 1983), 38.

11. Angela Calomiris, *Red Masquerade: Undercover for the FBI* (Philadelphia: J. B. Lippincott, 1950), 29.

12. Riis's introduction to *How the Other Half Lives: Studies among the Tenements of New York* (New York: Charles Scribner's Sons, 1889) sets the tone for his argument: "In the tenements all the influences make for evil; because they are the hot-beds of the epidemics that carry death to rich and poor alike; the nurseries of pauperism and crime that fill our jails and police courts; that throw off a scum of forty thousand human wrecks to the island asylums and workhouses year by year; that turned out in the last eight years a round half million beggars to prey upon our charities; that maintain a standing army of ten thousand tramps with all that that implies; because, above all, they touch the family life with deadly moral contagion"(3). If the tenements themselves are "prolific of untold depravities," their inhabitants are inevitably stamped by the same (8).

13. Joel Schwartz, *The New York Approach: Robert Moses, Urban Liberals, and Redevelopment of the Inner City* (Columbus: Ohio State University Press, 1993), 13, 46.

14. Ibid., 38, 42.

15. Stephany, "Interview with Aaron Siskind," 49.

16. Siskind typically shot his Feature Group images with a Voigtlander Avus, a 9 × 12 cm camera that required the use of cumbersome photographic plates as well as

a tripod and focusing hood. The equipment significantly slowed production and made it virtually impossible for the user to capture images without the subject's consent or at least awareness. For Siskind, who remained committed to the use of large-format apparatus throughout his career (against the trend toward 35 mm cameras, which were much smaller and faster to deploy), these properties were critical not only in producing more contemplative, formally self-conscious images, but also in conditioning the photographic contract between the documentary observer and his or her subjects.

17. These images, along with all Siskind's extant images from the projects *Portrait of a Tenement* and *Dead End: The Bowery,* are housed at the George Eastman House, Still Photograph Archive, Rochester, New York. Representative images are available online at "Photography Collections Online," George Eastman House, www.geh.org.

18. The Catholic Worker movement, dedicated to promotion of social justice through the teachings of the Catholic Church, was a fixture on the Lower East Side. It began in the form of the *Catholic Worker* journal (first published in 1933 and handed out for a penny an issue in Union Square and other downtown sites historically associated with labor activism) and took shape in two sites on the Lower East Side offering communal housing to those subscribing to its tenets. These communities were reliable sites of labor protest and war resistance. See Mark Zwick and Louise Zwick, "Blowing the Dynamite of the Church," in *The Catholic Worker Movement: Intellectual and Spiritual Origins* (Mahwah, NJ: Paulist Press, 2005), 1–29.

19. Siskind's emphasis on the tenement is a useful index of the ways in which his documentary practices evade such influential explications as William Stott's, in *Documentary Expression and Thirties America* (New York: Oxford University Press, 1973), of New Deal–era imaging. Unlike the FSA files, whose rhetoric and social logic Stott links to the production of the viewer's sympathy for subjects in need of recovery, Siskind's images seem constructed to resist such investments. His tenement dwellers have not been left behind by modernity. Rather, they are exemplary figures for it, and the photograph that documents the modes of social being they achieve itself becomes a space of encounter for the viewer. On the "excite[ment]" for documentarians of "the hitherto unimagined existence of workers, minorities, the rural, and the poor" as photographic subjects, see Stott, 134–35.

20. Stephany, "Interview with Aaron Siskind," 41.

21. Siskind, "Feature Group," reprinted in *Aaron Siskind: Toward a Personal Vision, 1935–1955,* ed. Deborah Marin Kao and Charles A. Meyer (Chestnut Hill, MA: Boston College Museum of Art, 1944), 28.

22. In this transcription of density, Siskind clearly draws on a longstanding tradition: what social historians call the "common culture" of New York City Jews, predicated on density as both an architectural fact and a social idea. Richard Plunz, in *A History of Housing in New York City* (New York: Columbia University Press, 1990), 132, describes the formative, even determinative, influence of density on the shaping of "Jewish culture" in downtown New York and beyond.

23. Stephany, "Interview with Aaron Siskind," 41.

24. Aaron Siskind, "The Drama of Objects," *Minicam Photography* 8, no. 9 (1945): 22.

25. Stephany, "Interview with Aaron Siskind," 41; Stryker, cited in Natanson, *The Black Image in the New Deal,* 58.

26. Allan Sekula, "The Body and the Archive," in *The Contest of Meaning: Critical Histories of Photography,* ed. Richard Bolton (Cambridge: MIT Press, 1992), 59, argues for the instrumentality of this image as a way of "*reclaiming* [Evans's] photographs from the various archival repositories which held copyright to or authority over his pictures," and also attests to Evans's resistance to the "proliferation" of photo-archival modes of disciplining social bodies "into the spaces of metropolitan life in the 1930s."

27. "Walker Evans: License Photo Studio, New York, 1934," Heilbrun Timeline of Art History, Metropolitan Museum of Art, www.metmuseum.org/toah/works-of-art/1972.742.17, accessed September 22, 2011.

28. Peter Galassi, *Walker Evans and Company* (New York: Museum of Modern Art, 2000) 161. Galassi also notes that this temporal collapse is "part of what makes [Evans's] work forward-looking," the reason why it "now seems closer to what has come after than to what came before."

29. Riis, *How the Other Half Lives* 104, is particularly devastating on Baxter Street as proleptic, historically and geographically, of the Lower East Side proper: "Baxter Street, with its interminable rows of old clothes shops and its brigades of pullers—ill-nicknamed the Bay in honor perhaps, of the tars who lay to there after a cruise to stock up their togs, or maybe after the 'schooners' of beer plentifully bespoke in that latitude—Bayard Street, with its synagogues and its crowds, gave us a foretaste of [Jewtown]."

30. Nick Tosches, *King of the Jews* (New York: Ecco, 2005), 122, 10.

31. Walker Evans, "The Reappearance of Photography," in Jeff L. Rosenheim and

Douglas Eklund, *Unclassified: A Walker Evans Anthology* (Zurich: Scalo, 2000). Originally published in *Hound & Horn* 5 (October–December 1931): 80.

32. Riis, *How the Other Half Lives,* 79. See also Tyler Anbinder, *Five Points: the 19th-Century New York City Neighborhood that Invented Tap Dance, Stole Elections, and Became the World's Most Notorious Slum* (New York: Plume, 2002).

33. See, for example, *Wooden House in Ossining, 1930; Roadside Stand near Birmingham, 1935; Roadside Store between Tuscaloosa and Greensboro, Alabama, 1936; Church of the Nazarene, Tennessee, 1936; Alabama Feed Store Front, 1936; Grocery Store, Greensboro, Alabama, 1935–6; Store in Marion, Alabama, 1936; Crossroads Store, Sprott, Alabama, 1935–6.*

34. Anzia Yezierska, "Brothers," in *How I Found America: Collected Stories of Anzia Yezierska,* ed. Vivian Gornick (New York: Persea Books, 1991), 193.

35. Abraham Cahan, *The Rise of David Levinsky* (New York: Modern Library, 2001), 93.

36. Henry Roth, *Call It Sleep* (New York: Farrar, Straus and Giroux, 1991), 174.

37. Shahn's photographic archive is held at the Harvard University Art Museums; a representative sampling of his work on the Lower East Side is available in the searchable collection database "Harvard Art Museums/Collection," at www.harvardartmuseums.org/collection/.

38. William Carlos Williams, "To Elsie," in *The Collected Poems of William Carlos Williams, Vol. 1: 1909–1939,* ed. Christopher MacGowan and A. Walton Litz (New York: New Directions, 1991), 218.

39. Cited in Joyce Antler, *You Never Call! You Never Write! A History of the Jewish Mother* (New York: Oxford University Press, 2008), 49.

40. Hasia Diner, *Lower East Side Memories: A Jewish Place in America* (Princeton: Princeton University Press, 2000), 100.

41. Walker Evans, quoted in John T. Hill and Jerry L. Thompson, eds., *Walker Evans at Work* (New York: Harper and Row, 1982), 151.

42. Deborah Martin Kao, Laura Katzman, and Jena Webster, *Ben Shahn's New York: The Photography of Modern Times* (Cambridge, MA: Harvard University Art Museums, 2000).

43. Richard Doud, interview with Ben Shahn, April 14, 1965, Smithsonian Archive of American Art. Available online at www.aaa.si.edu/collections/oralhistories/transcripts/shahn64.htm.

44. In his interview with Richard Doud (ibid.), Shahn notes: "I didn't trust the government facilities for even developing. I sent it in to New York"; more broadly, he notes, he "had this happy arrangement that I wasn't in the employ of Roy so he couldn't very well give me instructions, you see?"

45. Ibid.

46. Natanson, *The Black Image in the New Deal,* 92 (emphasis in the original). This effect is also found in Shahn's Lower East Side photographs of a Greek American and an African American man and the painting based on them; these images are reproduced in Kao, Katzman, and Webster, *Ben Shahn's New York,* 194–96.

47. The classic reading of the Brooklyn Bridge as an icon of American modernity is Alan Trachtenberg, *Brooklyn Bridge: Fact and Symbol* (Chicago: University of Chicago Press, 1979); notably, his reading turns centrally on Walker Evans's 1929 portfolio of images of the bridge, in which Evans first began to articulate the aesthetic and temporal logic that would define his work. On the Brooklyn Bridge as reimagined as part of the infrastructure of Jewish American flight, see Schwartz, *The New York Approach,* 14.

**With Trauma / Eric Rosenberg**

1. For an overview of Walker Evans's life and career, see Maria Morris Hambourg et al., *Walker Evans* (New York: Metropolitan Museum of Art, 2000); Belinda Rathbone, *Walker Evans: A Biography* (Boston: Mariner Books, 2000); and James R. Mellow, *Walker Evans* (New York: Basic Books, 2001).

2. See Wanda Corn, *The Great American Thing* (Berkeley: University of California Press, 2001), for the fullest recent account of transatlanticism in the 1920s.

3. For both agreement and disagreement with such a claim, see John Tagg, *The Burden of Representation* (Minneapolis: University of Minnesota Press, 1993), and *The Disciplinary Frame* (Minneapolis: University of Minnesota Press, 2009). Tagg's work on Evans unpacks more vigorously the ideological formations that shaped the conditions in which the photographer's work was produced.

4. Eric Rudway's *The Great Depression and the New Deal* (Oxford: Oxford University Press, 2008) is a concise and useful introduction to the historical situation both in the United States and globally.

5. The literature on trauma is vast and varied. Recent theoretical accounts of the condition, its symptoms, its affect, its treatment, and its interpretation in literary, his-

torical, art historical, and psychoanalytic discourses are covered in texts such as Cathy Caruth, *Unclaimed Experience: Trauma, Narrative, History* (Baltimore: Johns Hopkins University Press, 1996); Dominick LaCapra, *Writing History, Writing Trauma* (Baltimore: Johns Hopkins University Press, 2000); Ulrich Baer, *Spectral Evidence: The Photography of Trauma* (Cambridge, MA: MIT Press, 2005); and Lisa Saltzman and Eric Rosenberg, eds., *Trauma and Visuality in Modernity* (Hanover, NH: University Press of New England, 2006).

6. See Molly Nesbitt, *Atget's Seven Albums* (New Haven: Yale University Press, 1992).

7. See Heinrich Wölfflin, *The Principles of Art History,* trans. M. D. Hottinger (New York: Dover Publications, 1950), first published in German in 1915.

8. Leslie Katz, "Interview with Walker Evans," *Art in America,* March–April 1971, 85.

9. See James Elkins, *Photography Theory* (London: Routledge, 2007), for discussions by leading critics, theorists, and historians of the current status of photography's interpretation.

10. This is what John Tagg has so aptly called the disciplinary frame (see n. 3 above).

11. Lenore Terr's *Too Scared To Cry: Psychic Trauma in Childhood* (New York: Basic Books, 1992) offers a particularly trenchant account of the dismemberment of time in trauma.

12. The obvious argument with my claim is Picasso's *Guernica.* See T. J. Clark, "Part 6: Mural," *Picasso and Truth,* Mellon Lectures, National Gallery of Art, 2009, available at www.nga.gov/podcasts/.

13. My argument runs blatantly counter to that of Steve Spence in "Van Gogh in Alabama, 1936," *Representations* 75 (Summer 2001): 33–60. Spence offers a cogent and fascinating analysis of Evans's interest in modern art exhibitions in New York and the place of a certain modernist history of art in the photographer's practice as he produced many of the images that would appear in *American Photographs* (New York: Museum of Modern Art, 1938) and *Let Us Now Praise Famous Men* (Boston: Houghton Mifflin, 1941).

14. *Factory Street*'s irresolution is even more striking given its great formal and pictorial debt to Eugène Atget's *Coin de la rue Valette et Panthéon* (1925).

15. Tagg, *The Burden of Representation,* 183.

16. I treat something of photography's inherent violence in my essay "Photography Is Over, If You Want It," in *The Meaning of Photography,* ed. Robin Kelsey and Blake Stimson (New Haven: Yale University Press, 2008). A more seminal consideration of

this issue can be found in Susan Sontag, *Regarding the Pain of Others* (New York: Picador, 2004).

17. Tagg reproduces and aims his discussion in part at an Evans photograph, *Railroad Station, Edwards, Mississippi,* 1936, inviting much consideration in terms of my argument, as will emerge later in this book.

18. See Eric Rosenberg, "Walker Evans's Depression and the Trauma of Photography," in Saltzman and Rosenberg, *Trauma and Visuality in Modernity,* 28–47.

19. Lincoln Kirstein, "Photographs of America: Walker Evans," *American Photographs* (New York: Museum of Modern Art, 1938), 194.

20. Judith Herman, *Trauma and Recovery* (New York: Basic Books, 1997).

21. Neil Hertz, "The Notion of Blockage in the Literature of the Sublime," in *The End of the Line* (New York: Columbia University Press, 1985), 39–58.

22. Here I differ considerably with John Tagg in my reading of this photograph and its characteristic motives. Tagg accounts for the image (and others like it) in terms of realism as ideology, the mobilization of the dream experience, and wish fulfillment. I prefer to see works like *Railroad Station, Factory Town,* and *General Store* as disabling the possibility of dreamwork, perhaps even of ideology, and thus, in part, their disturbance rather than caress of the eye. Tagg would seem to find the photograph eminently suitable to the possibility of narrative. I am less comfortable with this implication. See Tagg, *The Burden of Representation,* 183.

23. See, of course, Roland Barthes, *Camera Lucida: Reflections on Photography* (New York: Hill and Wang, 1982) and Geoffrey Batchen, ed., *Photography Degree Zero: Reflections on Roland Barthes's Camera Lucida* (Cambridge, MA: MIT Press, 2009).

24. See Babette Rothschild, *The Body Remembers: The Psychophysiology of Trauma and Trauma Treatment* (New York: W. W. Norton, 2000).

25. *The WPA Guide to 1930s Alabama* (Tuscaloosa: University of Alabama Press, [1941] 2000), 84.

26. "The History of Edwards," Town of Edwards, Mississippi, website, 2009, www.townofedwards.com/history.htm.

27. Richard F. Weingroff, "US Route 80: The Dixie Overland Highway," in *Highway History,* Federal Highway Administration, U.S. Department of Transportation, 2009, www.fhwa.dot.gov/infrastructure/us80.cfm,.

28. Fredric Jameson, *The Political Unconscious: Narrative as a Socially Symbolic Act* (Ithaca, NY: Cornell University Press, 1981), 102.

29. *WPA Guide to 1930s Alabama,* 312.

30. See John H. Blitz, *Moundville* (Tuscaloosa: University of Alabama Press, 2008). Excavations and archaeological work were carried out in the area throughout the 1930s, and interest in the local ancient Native American burial mounds dated back to the middle of the nineteenth century. By the late 1920s the Alabama Museum of National History was buying portions of the area. Mound State Park was established in 1933 and Mound State Monument in 1938. In a paper titled "The Indian Mounds at Moundville, Tuscaloosa County," the museum's director argued: "We robbed the Indians of everything they had, and the least we can do is preserve this wonderful monument which they left behind" (quoted in ibid., 20). According to Blitz, "Depression excavations resulted in the excavation of 75 house remains, 2050 burials and thousands of artifacts" (ibid.). Ironically, the area was affected deeply by the Depression, and local laborers, hungry for work, were frequently enlisted to help with the excavations, meant to restore some sense of narrative and presence to a previously eviscerated local demographic.

31. *WPA Guide to 1930s Alabama,* 312.

32. Eudora Welty, "Death of a Traveling Salesman," in *A Curtain of Green and Other Stories* (Orlando, FL: Harcourt, 1941), 231–53.

33. Ibid., 233.

34. Ibid., 232.

35. Ibid, 233–34.

# Index

*Page numbers in italics refer to illustrations.*

University of California Press, one of the most distinguished university presses in the United States, enriches lives around the world by advancing scholarship in the humanities, social sciences, and natural sciences. Its activities are supported by the UC Press Foundation and by philanthropic contributions from individuals and institutions. For more information, visit www.ucpress.edu.



University of California Press
Berkeley and Los Angeles, California

University of California Press, Ltd.
London, England



Library of Congress Cataloging-in-Publication Data

Blair, Sara.
Trauma and documentary photography of the FSA / Sara Blair, Eric Rosenberg.
p. cm. — (Defining moments in American photography ; 5)
Includes bibliographical references and index.
ISBN 978-0-520-26565-3 (hardback) — ISBN 978-0-520-26566-0 (paper)
1. Documentary photography—United States—History—20th century. 2. United States—Economic conditions—1918–1945—Pictorial works. 3. United States—Social conditions—1933–1945—Pictorial works. 4. United States. Farm Security Administration. I. Rosenberg, Eric II. Title.
TR820.5.B58 2012
770.973—dc23 2011043600

Manufactured in the United States of America

21 20 19 18 17 16 15 14 13 12
10 9 8 7 6 5 4 3 2 1

The paper used in this publication meets the minimum requirements of ANSI/NISO Z39.48–1992 (R 1997) *(Permanence of Paper).*

Designer: Nola Burger
Text: 10.75/14 Granjon
Display: Interstate
Compositor: Integrated Composition Systems
Prepress: iocolor
Indexer: Andrew Joron
Printer and binder: Thomson-Shore, Inc.